TRINITY OF LEADERSHIP

Learners, Thinkers, Tinkerers

Trisha Beck and Denise Nelson Nash

Contributing Authors: Sharon Counts, Michael Miller, Herminio L. Perez, and Lucas Welter

Published by Akers Follett Press, New York

ISBN: 979-8-9947648-0-0

Cover design and image by Andy Magee

The pause symbol is represented by two vertical, parallel lines set against a sunset over ocean waves. These lines are echoed by two parallel rocks in the sea, bringing together a trinity of sun, sea, and land as metaphors for learners, thinkers, and tinkerers. It's an abstract interpretation of *pause and reflect* expressed through the mandala form

Developmental Editor Wordy Wives

Disclaimer

The stories and examples in this book are based on real experiences. Names and identifying details have been changed to protect the privacy of individuals. Any resemblance to actual persons or actual events is purely coincidental.

This book is designed to provide information and inspiration to readers about leadership. The content reflects the personal experiences and perspectives of the authors and should not be used as a substitute for consultation with professional advisors in organizational development, human resources, or related fields.

First Edition: March 2026

Printed in the United States of America

For the ones who moved us forward, mentored us toward growth,
led us onward, and continue to love us fiercely.

***

The Learner asks the questions. The Thinker creates space for
those questions to breathe. The Tinkerer experiments with answers.
And the journey continues, each time with deeper wisdom and with
greater impact.

Contents

Preface

In 2020, a pandemic and subsequent chaos and crisis spread throughout the globe. The world went on pause. At the same time, a cohort of accomplished cross-sector professionals was on an academic journey together, and this is where our story, as the co-authors of this book, begins.

New York City. May 10, 2025. Rosa Mexicano Restaurant.

Six of us gathered around a table crackling with anticipation. You could feel it — standing on a threshold, knowing something significant was about to happen.

We had invited our friends to join us on a book-writing journey— something none of those around the table had done before. They came because they trusted us. Not because we had a perfect plan or a guaranteed path to publication, but because in our Circle of Trust, we had learned that the best discoveries happen when you're willing to venture onto unfamiliar roads together.

Michael, the storyteller. Lucas, the ideator. Herminio, the humanist. Sharon, the cultivator. And us, the co-authors and organizers, who believed this circle of individuals could become something more.

This book emerged from our shared academic journey, from the circle we formed, from the conversations before and after dinner, from the trust we built by showing up as learners even when the world expected us to be experts. What you hold in your hands is not just our individual insights, but the collective wisdom of six people willing to connect the dots forward together.

Two visionaries, Drs. Lisette Nieves and Noel Anderson, co-founders of the New York University EdD Leadership and Innovation program, brought us together. The program reinforced that leadership is a journey — a journey of discovering and uncovering what lies beneath.

We learned to set aside assumptions and truly see what was in front of us. We learned to think more expansively and deeply. We recommitted ourselves to being Learners and Thinkers. And we tinkered.

We tinkered with concepts, approaches, thoughts, data, and perspectives. Along the way, we forged lifelong friendships, tested big ideas, and reconfirmed our commitment to transformative partnerships, forging meaningful impact. Together, we became the leaders our complex world needs — practitioners who think like scholars, scholars who act like practitioners, and change agents who understand that our greatest challenges require connected solutions. This was the gift given to us, and now we share this gift with you in *Trinity of Leadership: Learners, Thinkers, and Tinkerers*, a book about the journey, not the destination.

Trisha Beck and Denise Nelson Nash
March 2026

Introduction

What if everything you know about leadership prepared you for the past?

Wait, what?! What about the present and the future?

In today's ever-changing and often chaotic times, how do you prepare to be the dynamic leader of the future? Who are you today, and who will you need to be in the future?

In a rapidly evolving world, yesterday's leadership approaches or models no longer guarantee tomorrow's success. Tomorrow's most dynamic leaders will foster continuous learning, embrace adaptability, and recognize that success in times of uncertainty depends on the ability to connect, grow, and evolve. Leaders must do more than adapt—they must navigate uncertainty, reinvent to drive innovation, and create meaningful impact. It's about the leadership journey, not merely a destination of frameworks, strategies, and descriptions of leadership styles.

Our beginning

The Trinity project began with an invitation to the Circle of Trust (how we characterize our group), inviting them to a "classified opportunity that requires the utmost discretion; and yes, this message will self-destruct after reading (just kidding, but wouldn't that be amazing?)." We went on to describe our goal: "We're assembling a carefully curated circle of trusted thought leaders and brilliant minds for a project to demystify the leadership landscape. This isn't just another leadership project; we're crafting something to challenge the tralatious and explore the unwritten. If you're intrigued, and we hope you are, please join us on March 20, 2025, at 8 pm ET."

In that meeting, we asked ourselves:

- If you had to name what has most significantly impacted or shaped who you are as a leader today, what would it be?
- When you think about your leadership journey, what were the defining moments that got you to where you are today?
- How do we equip visionary leaders for the future, building on past principles while adapting to new realities?

Our unifying principles

We took a connective approach to developing this book. The authors began by meeting for ideatorium sessions. First, as a group, asking ourselves these questions, then engaging in small group discussions around what it means to be a Learner, Thinker, and Tinkerer. What emerged were themes of immeasurable aspects of leadership. There are plenty of "how-to" books; what we aim to share are the intangibles—that which is not easily measurable: trust, empathy, and learning—the key(s) to being and becoming the human-centered leader of the future.

Our approach

Next was the approach. We focused on leveraging our collective years of personal stories and narratives to explore deeper leadership qualities. Those characteristics that transform people into better human beings, not just better leaders. We paired off with a chaptermate to develop content that told a story to inspire and motivate while navigating uncertainty.

Sharon Counts reveals an idea that will resonate with many in "Strong and Wrong." "In the performing arts, there's an expression about how performers make choices on stage, meaning how they express the intention of a gesture, movement, or word. These choices are how an actor brings a character to life, making them specific and unique, and are based on their understanding of the character's objectives, obstacles, and motivations. The expression is "strong and wrong," which means fully committing to the choice, whatever it may be.

In "The Set Up," Michael Miller shares a story that is familiar to us all — the disappointment after expectations aren't met. "The

Emperor-with-no-clothes arrived to much fanfare in our organization. It was a long-awaited appointment, and this individual simply oozed charisma and leadership experience. Everyone was thrilled and excited. The possibilities were endless."

In "The Questions," Trisha Beck recounts learning from someone who really impacted her life. It was her first leadership role, and she was determined to rise to the challenge and meet the CEO's expectations. "About once a month, he would show up in my office. With each visit came the questions: "Why do we...?" "Why don't we...?" "Can we do this better or differently?" Always questions I couldn't answer. I would reluctantly respond, "I'm not sure."

"The Invitation" by Denise Nelson Nash paints a vivid picture of living, learning, and leading in another country — another culture. She learned, "similar" was not the "same." "The moment of "similar" wasn't "same" wasn't really a moment, it was more of a gradual shift of recognition and realization. It was then that my leadership learning journey accelerated. Living internationally within another culture required me to observe, adapt, and learn constantly."

The Trinity

The Learner, the Thinker, the Tinkerer: which resonates with you? Where is your sweet spot? As you reflect on your leadership of yesterday and today, would your response change? Leveraging the trinity concept, each chapter will challenge you to get comfortable in each of these spaces. How are you a Learner? When are you a Thinker? What does it mean to be a Tinkerer?

As you read the Trinity of Leadership, we challenge you to pause and reflect: Are you truly learning something each day or are you coasting along? Do you carve out time to think deeply and challenge your assumptions? How boldly do you tinker and challenge the status quo? Pick up the book with intention. Set the book aside with purpose. Find a Trinity partner. How will you embrace the journey together? Let our stories ignite your revelations. Share your breakthroughs. Voice your struggles. Break the mold of the leader you are today as you rise to be the leader of tomorrow.

Lucas Welter reflects on his introduction to "Tell me more" — an elegant way of saying you have no idea what to ask next. It was on a flight from Los Angeles to Denver when he was in his twenties. He was seated next to a woman in her early seventies who was curious about Lucas' Brazilian heritage. After the usual polite airplane diplomacy, he found himself telling her more as the border between personal and personal-ish began to blur. She led with curiosity, and he followed with answers. Since that encounter, "Tell me more" has become his way of expressing consent-based curiosity. Just as his seatmate on the flight decided how far to go and he followed, he has come to recognize that leadership isn't the authority to answer; it's the courage to inquire, to make room for someone else's story to land.

Herminio L. Perez shares a story about an unexpected job loss and the fears many of us share: Am I still employable? Is it too late to start over? Rather than surrendering to uncertainty, he talks about how the circumstances were reframed and what felt like a forced retirement turned into an opportunity for reinvention. By leveraging an academic background, professional expertise, and hard-earned reputation, the story reminds us that embarking on a creative new path driven by passion and purpose is possible. The journey reminds us that career disruption, even late in life, can become the catalyst for our most meaningful chapter yet.

As we embarked on our journey, you, the reader, are now embarking on yours. Just as we committed to generously sharing our experiences to guide and support your Trinity journey, we challenged ourselves to break through the barriers of vulnerability and fear. We didn't just give ourselves permission to be brave; we gave ourselves the freedom to explore and reflect on our own Trinity journey. This freedom resulted in a transformative energy that propelled us forward. Now that freedom and energy await you.

We are thrilled to have you join us on this leadership journey. We invite you to embrace the discovery. Remain ready to dismantle your assumptions. Give yourself permission to be vulnerable. Welcome the freedom to explore. Challenge the fear. Be courageous and brave. Prepare for the evolutionary leap to your future leadership identity.

Connecting the Dots

The connect-the-dot puzzle; scattered dots that make no sense. You choose your starting point and follow the journey of the dots until the hidden image appears. The image that was there all along. You just had to connect the dots to see it.

Looking back at the dots that shaped our past, each of us sees different images and has walked different paths. The "dots" of our beginnings differed, but we arrived at the same truth. Leadership is learning, thinking, and tinkering. Once you embrace that, it is liberating. As you embark on this journey, when you begin to connect not just our dots but your own, the image will appear. We will show you how we discovered it. You see, the journey is continuous. The learning never ends. The highway stretches infinitely ahead. And that's not a problem to solve. That's the whole point.

PART ONE

THE LEARNER

CHAPTER ONE:

The Stories That Shape Us

Michael Miller

Cue the Spotlight

Like one of those Hollywood cinema techniques from the '30s and '40s, where lighting was used to isolate stars with halos, I saw Michael across a crowded room. It was as if the director had cued "make the surrounding room disappear." I crossed the room and told him, "I want to know you"—or perhaps I said "I need to know you." The fact that he didn't find an excuse to extract himself—but instead smiled, extended his hand, and said, "Well, let's start now"—tells you exactly who Michael is. He is the kind of person others instinctively trust: a connector with rare insight and authenticity. Six years later, I am grateful that he didn't run away from me. Having his voice and his wisdom in this book felt not just important, but inevitable

-Denise Nelson Nash

Once you really embrace the idea that you're never going to be 'done' learning how to lead it is liberating. You can stop pretending you have all the answers. You can make mistakes. You can be curious instead of certain.

Storytelling as the Foundation

First and foremost, I consider myself a storyteller. It's the easiest way to encapsulate who I am and how I move through the world. Storytelling is ancient and connects human beings in ways that have lasted millennia. Simply think of a story that you'll never forget. It doesn't particularly matter what the story was about, but something about the way it was told, the details, was it humorous? Devastating? Did it make you furious? Was it even a satisfying outcome? Did the people involved, and their experience, have an impact on you? We are surrounded by stories, both fictional and not, every day. Stories come in many forms -- we even consume one another's "stories" on Instagram and Tik Tok hundreds (more?) of times a day. In books like these, successful authors communicate their knowledge and lessons through stories. While checklists and bullet points can list traits and behaviors one should think about, shift, put in place, or practice, many times we don't understand them in our core. We get the concept, but it can be difficult for us to engage with them in the moment or naturally -- oftentimes feeling overwhelmed by "trying" too many of the lessons all at once in a situation or conversation. It doesn't come quickly or naturally; you get frustrated and go back to what "works" or feels comfortable. Ultimately, I want you to intrinsically change the way you see your own practice every day. It's a process of... here it comes... learning.

We cannot possibly know everything there is to know in any given situation -- we bring our lived experiences and knowledge and do the best we can. However, those things can be utilized in different ways with different effects. We can change the way we approach a situation - for instance, in a meeting with several people who report to you - what if your answer to a question that was difficult or even pressing was "I don't know" or "I will need to get back to you on that"? So often we feel we need to have all the answers to convey (or portray) strong leadership. The idea that we've got to always be strong or right or powerful in business, whatever that business may be, is learned. Where might these ideas come from? Well, we've been told through, you guessed it, stories. Stories told from coworkers, stories from keynote speakers, stories in books, and probably most often from film and television.

Take a moment to think about the way a "boss" behaves in the media. What is your memory of how bosses behave in film and television that you've seen over the years? What attributes do you connect to those in power? Many times, we think of the classic evil-boss archetype. They don't care about their employees, just the bottom line. They don't listen particularly well, they don't like to be told "no," they don't like to hear about data or news that contradict the next big plan. Your family doesn't matter. It's Christmas Eve? Get me that report now! The list goes on and on -- and even in many cases the stories are satirical, comedic, or even far-fetched, we still consume examples that are much simpler, quieter, and more consistent every day.

We want you to begin to think about your career and leadership journey as traveling a sort of "cerebral highway." Let's take a moment to marinate on this notion. It's not the destination; it's the journey. No matter the exit you take or the speed that you drive, remember the learning happens in the doing. The learning is not the result. The off-ramp is simply the continuation of the journey but on a different road- it might be off the beaten path, it might be a bit longer, it might be a little bumpier. It's not which off-ramp you choose; it's learning the twists and curves of the road less taken or discovering where a new road needs to be constructed. There is no GPS or navigation system to make yourself a better leader -- it would be unhelpful and frankly, dangerous, to let that guide us. Leadership is active and participatory.

We think we're driving toward a destination called "Good Boss" or "Good Leader," but the highway doesn't end. Every exit is just another on-ramp. The journey isn't continuous because we're slow learners--- it's continuous because the world keeps changing, and so do we. If you were to think back to a film or a television show you saw as a young person -- gosh, young person, how old do I sound? You would almost surely be able to recall the "boss" character. Now, this character might be a "good" boss or a "bad" boss, but regardless, you would be able to answer questions about what makes one a "good" or "bad" boss in terms of what we see on the screen. If you're a fan of Hallmark Christmas movies, you'll have some of the best worst examples of stereotypical bosses who push their staff too far and the staff must reclaim some kind of personal balance to understand the spirit of Christmas... or something like that. My point is that we are constantly bombarded with ideas, images, and representations of what a boss is. It doesn't matter much if it's positive or negative, true or false, it's just important to know that it's happening frequently in the media. On the side of real-life bosses -- well, this can be a bit trickier. We are often let into the world of corporate leaders when they make big decisions. Think Mark Zuckerberg, Elizabeth Holmes, Musk. Why do you know these people? What do you think of them? How are they/have they been portrayed to us in the public eye? I would argue that most people can't name many Fortune 500 company leaders -- maybe Bob Iger from Disney, he's in the press a lot, right?

Meet the Archetypes

I'd like to introduce you to three "bosses" or leaders that have shaped my career, sense of self in the workplace and many, many, many times solidified the type of leader I refuse to be. Meet Mr. Indecisive, the Emperor with no clothes, and the Egoist (cue scary music, thunder & lightning). It doesn't matter where or when I or you may have worked for or with this crew -- what is important is what we learned from them, how their actions -- or in Mr. Indecisive's case, lack thereof -- shaped the organizations they held power in and the people that worked for them. Sadly, most people have far fewer examples of model bosses in their careers. I have had only a handful of excellent, shining examples of leadership in the workplace -- while that may seem sad, it's really wonderful to know it's possible and to see the incredible productivity and community that can exist and thrive in a well-led office or business.

Let's begin with Mr. (or Ms.) Indecisive, shall we? Mr. Indecisive was a nice person. One of the nicest, in fact. So nice. Like, so nice that you questioned why is this person being so nice? Well, if you never decide, if you never pick a position, if you never commit, you won't make people mad because you won't promise something you won't deliver on. It's also easier to do nothing many times. Not all the time, but when you have people working for you who must decide, then your decisions are made for you. Take this example – you work in a tight-knit group at work. There are a few of you who run the organization day-to-day and behind the scenes, you're doing most of the heavy lifting or implementing the decisions from higher up. One of your administrative colleagues is harassed or verbally assaulted by another employee… Everything in your organization's Human Resources policy or handbook has clear ways of dealing with such an incident. Mr. Indecisive is told about this incident and rightly, is dismayed and angered by it. As he should be; one of his key team members has been treated abysmally. Now what – take a second to think about what *you* might do as a first step to resolve the situation. There are a few ways one might approach this; however, doing *nothing* or saying you will and doing nothing is… problematic. Speaking with both employees, referring the matter to HR, etc. But lip-service and no action does a few things – first and foremost it erodes the trust and the relationship you have with your employee who was wronged and whom you have to work with and rely on every day. You now become unreliable and frankly, weak when it comes to serious problem-solving. The employee, consciously or unconsciously, now knows that this behavior is acceptable or, at the very least, is ignored. One's indecision to act has created organizational rot to set in. Pair all this with the regular indecision occurring daily – do we have a meeting about that problem? Maybe. Should we spend funds on this project or that one? Not sure, I'll get back to you. All of this is insidious. Eventually, senior staff start making decisions on their own – the people closest to the problem often have the answer – and they use their best judgment to keep the organization on-track. If you were in this position, what would you do to improve or change the culture of your indecisive leader?

And since you've hired brilliant people, then most or all of "your" decisions are excellent ones that allow the organization to flourish or at least stay moving forward. The leader who can't decide is a weak leader – you will learn very quickly that while those around the leader, those in the organization who had some distance, *like* Mr. Indecisive they don't actually *respect* him. We have to learn to make choices both large and small, insignificant and major and LEARN from them. We need the experience of moving forward. If we don't, we're stuck and so is the organization.

The Emperor-with-no-clothes arrives to much fanfare to your organization. It's been a long-awaited appointment and this individual simply oozes charisma and leadership experience. Everyone is thrilled and excited. The possibilities are endless. Turns out, the Emperor (or Empress) possesses mostly insecurity and lack of real-world experience; they have very little interest in learning anything about the organization or its people; a real recipe for disaster. Changes are made quickly with little institutional understanding. Major systems are ripped out from the root with such speed that everyone's head is spinning because of the rush to make a mark. All the while, the Emperor's vision is continually touted as the "only" and "foolproof" way to innovate and improve the organization. A major takeaway for us all is you must be patient with change. You must build a coalition. You must treat people as the experts they are -- those who work in the organization you have walked into have so much institutional knowledge. You can't download patience. You can't hack wisdom. You can't magic change. It's like a garden - some things only come from showing up, season after season, especially when nothing seems to be growing.

What did I learn? If things aren't "growing" for you as a leader – don't resort to drastic measures first. Yes, you're the new one in town who has been hired to change and shape an organization... but if you don't get people on board with you, if you don't share your vision in detail – no matter how exciting and shiny the Cliff's Notes version is -- you'll lose your organization. Also, pro-tip, don't pit the staff against one another and don't disrespect what someone does in their current position. While all this sounds like just don't be a tyrant, yes, that's very true, there are specific things you can avoid doing so that people won't actually think you're some gorgon from a bad nightmare. Small, daily choices compound – like choosing curiosity over certainty in one meeting, admitting ignorance in another. These micro-moments matter more than macro-strategies. You are the new leader – you cannot possibly know everything – be patient to make decisions on the state of things. It's a long game. If you think six months is enough for major institutional change, you're probably wrong. Especially if you don't lift the hood and take a serious look at how that engine is assembled. And, in my case, changes made *against* the advice of people who know better leads to cleanup that lasts for years. Your choices as a leader matter. Check your ego at the door for a bit, no one wants to deal with it and, as I'll tell you next, you might just lose your entire business because of it.

Let me tell you about the Egoist, a good example of learning versus unlearning. A particularly unpleasant breed of leader. The Egoist has started their own company on the backs of others around them – friends and close colleagues. The company gains a respectable amount of success. Soon, the company flourishes and the Egoist has become so comfortable as the figurehead of the organization they now are quite comfortable treating all those friends and original crew as their underlings. They do the work; the Egoist takes the credit. The Egoist behaves as though no one can do it better... or at all, frankly. This is a particularly nasty trait. Because of the success of the company, they are now seen as an expert. To make matters worse, they are also quite adept in public settings and are quite charming. Yet, in the office, they always have a snide comment about your performance; they make critiques personal all the while exposing their insecurities to their staff. Let's also say this particular organization serves a population that is vulnerable or impressionable. The mission is to serve these young people and prepare them for the world outside of the organization's walls. The mistreated staff across the organization are deeply attached to the mission, and this population – so much so, that they put up with the Egoist's behavior more than they should. So the organization continues to crumble slowly; the erosion is undetectable at first. The Egoist contributes to the downfall in two major ways: they don't ensure there are checks and balances in their governance structure, and they push their talent away. This is often accomplished by a slow drip of belittlement, vanity, and folly.

I know this seems like an impossible situation. In fact, you may not be able to stop the organization's impending doom. But you have picked up our book! I put it to you that it's the open willingness to unlearn – a regular practice, not the specific unlearning of things or ideas. Much of our book is about changing the way you see yourself in relationship to your leadership, its style, content, and those around you. You're not a solo act, and the people you work with, for, or collaborate with aren't solo acts either. No matter what you think, business is a multi-player game. It's a human enterprise, and without effective, thoughtful interpersonal interactions, we're not going to get very far — or we'll just have to settle for mediocrity. The Egoist didn't learn anything until it was too late. Poor hiring decisions, top talent had fled the company, and new partners were brought in to save the finances. Turns out when you're a tyrant to everyone, and they own the majority stake in your company, they can fire you if they get tired of your... crap. The Egoist teaches us a few key things: if you surround yourself with yes-men, you'll be yes-ed to death — literally or figuratively. Hire people more skilled than you and treat them like the experts they are. Do not be led by ego; make sure you have a board or partner that can say "no" to you; "bad move" or "let's wait," etc.

When we think about what we have learned as good or bad leadership behavior, we often see it in relation to treating others poorly (bad), recognizing humanity in others (good), pushing too hard (bad), and making decisions without proper information (also, bad). But really at the end of the day, it's so many other interactions or decisions, small things, that really impact the way we are perceived and received by others. Are you thought of as fair? Patient? All of these traits or qualities are directly tied to our leadership impact. Small, daily choices compound---like choosing curiosity over certainty in one meeting, admitting ignorance in another. These micro-moments matter more than macro-strategies.

Humility in Leadership

Think for a moment about the best leaders or examples of leadership you have experienced or admired. Take a second to really analyze the traits of that person or their actions – what was it that allowed them to do what they did? Would you describe the actor or actions in your scenario as selfish, self-centered, or impulsive? What often is described as "weakness" by some is, in truth, one of the strongest leadership traits we have in our arsenal. The leader who is more concerned about optics – which, by the way, can be very important, often fails at their task. The leader who listens and admits that they don't know everything, that they need input from others to make decisions, those are the real change-makers who have a lasting impact on an organization or its people. In my experience, it really does feel like many leaders have no comprehension of the enormity of humility and kindness in the world of work. It's no secret that I've had more terrible bosses than good ones, but that doesn't mean that it's not possible to learn from the bad bosses as much as it is from the good bosses.

Those of us that have a calling to lead organizations and be transformative in our work. That's all very well and good, but there's a responsibility there, and one of those responsibilities is to treat your colleagues with dignity and respect. One of the ways that you do that, and arguably the easiest, is to treat them as human beings and to approach your work with humility. Recognizing that you don't know everything. You are fallible; you can make mistakes. Your human nature as a boss is not something that you can wish away or hide or disappear. In fact, those who try to do that are in real trouble.

The Human-Centric Nature of Leadership

"Leadership is a human business. *Period*." Whether you agree with me or not, it's true. The machines haven't completely taken over... yet. So, for now, you have to deal with other humans to get things done. And if that stresses you out or annoys you... well, you're not alone. Many people are in leadership because they were placed or appointed there. (If you'd like a somewhat glib but interesting take on this phenomenon, read The Peter Principle.) What I hope you take from this book – mainly – is that you must engage in a meaningful way with your colleagues and employees. Otherwise, it will be pointless for so many people – maybe not today, but tomorrow or the next day. Think about friends of yours who hate their boss or their job – maybe even another coworker. Why? What is it that drives them crazy about these people or places? I would put money on the idea that they are not conducive to a human-centered environment. What do I mean by this? Work that isn't rewarded or recognized. Most people just want to feel like they are contributing, that their work means something. You would be surprised how this simple concept could radically change a workplace or your more directly, your leadership. Not everyone wants to be the boss or even the center of attention. Most people want to go to work and feel that what they are doing, no matter what it is, is contributing to the mission and that it's valued by the people in "power." If you can give that to your colleagues or employees – you've basically won the battle.

Learning How to Learn

Because this isn't a how-to manual, you may be asking at this point, okay... so what? What can this guy actually tell me? Well, getting out of our own way is tricky. It's a process that honestly is about learning how to learn – how you learn, more specifically. The fact that you may even be willing to look at your learning style is a pretty big deal. By the way, this all isn't easy. It's not downloaded from the sky, nor does all of it come naturally to most of us. That's why there is school, and smart people who teach us things. You wouldn't have this book if you knew it all, and I wouldn't have gotten three degrees if I did too. So – where does that leave us? Right, learning to learn. Really, what I'm trying to impart to you is all of the above sections. You have to drop into your mind and begin actively going on the quest of learning how to make your leadership style different and impactful. Some of it may only need a little polishing.

I needed a lot of work on what I thought other people thought about me. What if they don't like what I said or did? What if they get... cue the scary music... mad at me? Oh, it's so exhausting to think how much time of my early professional career I spent worrying. Yet, here we are, and thankfully, I realized how ineffective it was. It happens when I first start teaching a class. It happens when I go into a room of executives. It happens all the time when someone asks me to describe my doctoral research. My brain short-circuits for a second, and I blank on any kind of skill or experience I possess. I used to *really* worry I wasn't capable of handling serious or stressful situations at work. The ironic part of all of this is that for years I could get on a stage in front of hundreds and thousands of people, singing and dancing and never feel insecure. Instead it was joyful and exhilarating. When I left the theater, I didn't connect the value of my training and experiences to leadership. But ex-perience after experience, new boss after new boss, it was impossible to escape that I was uniquely prepared to bring all of myself to my work.

This is your truth too. If you can dig deep, access but also honor the things that make you uniquely you.

I will give you an example. Not too long ago, a student of mine was having a tough time at school. Life was really throwing everything it could at them, and their schoolwork and attendance were suffering because of it. Tanking actually. The student – a great kid, by the way, super smart and absolutely capable – was now getting the reputation of being a "problem" and "difficult." Long story short, the student needed help and was lashing out at anyone and everyone they could to get a different response or result from where they were constantly finding themselves. It was referred to me as a behavioral problem. I knew how fierce this student could be – they were an excellent advocate for themselves, but sometimes didn't play fair – they said things and did things that didn't help their case or endear them to those who might help. A meeting was called with my boss and a few other people. It was a powder keg situation. I lost sleep worrying. I knew this student wasn't "bad" and yet they weren't helping their own case much. I didn't know what I was going to do in that room. After several days of serious fretting and stress, I had a moment of clarity: you can make this situation better; you can advocate for this student *and* give them some tough love *and* help them succeed. You can also keep the tone relatively neutral and keep things moving. I just dropped into the power and skills I knew I possessed. Suddenly I understood my quirky, "odd," "artsy" background was my super power. What the heck had I been doing for the last 20 years or so but preparing for moments like this?

In the end, the student appreciated being treated with respect; my boss was pleased it didn't descend into chaos; and there was a clear plan to move forward. The temperature was turned way down, and the student and I had a much stronger relationship that has continued to this day.

Case Study Approach Without Prescribed Problem

Here's the thing about most leadership books -- they love their case studies. You know the type: "Jennifer faced a difficult employee situation. She applied the SMART goal framework, had a crucial conversation using the 7-step method, and voilà! Problem solved, promotion earned, and probably a standing ovation from the board."

But that's not how it works, is it?

Real leadership moments are messier, sometimes smaller, and almost always unexpected. They're the Friday 4:47 pm email that ruins your weekend. They're the meetings where you realize halfway through that you've been solving the wrong problem for six months. They're the moment when your best employee tells you they're leaving, and you realize you never really knew what motivated them in the first place. It's the realization no one else has the institutional knowledge they had, and you're in trouble.

So, let's try something different. I'm going to share some situations – real ones, with the identifying details changed – and I'm not going to tell you what to do about them. Heck, I'm not even going to tell you what I did about them, or whether it worked. Because the point isn't the answer. The point is learning to sit with the questions, to recognize the patterns, and to develop your own instincts rather than download someone else's.

Let's say a stellar performer on your team hasn't been so stellar lately. Their work is still acceptable, but the spark is gone. Cue the myriad of questions one might ask themself: Do I address it? When do I address it, if I choose to? What if they have a sick parent? Or are they going through a divorce? Do I wait? Well, now their mediocre work and shift in attitude are affecting team morale. Now, do I act? And if I do, what do I address? There's no budget for raises this year, so I can't use the promotion card. Does that matter? I know people want recognition before money in many cases... What do I do?

Turns out, each person reading this book may have a different approach. And that's okay. The critical step here is not to question and go down the proverbial rabbit hole. Trust yourself and your instinct. If you get it wrong, you'll need to deal with the consequences. Inaction, however, the "I'll deal with it later" approach brings back our old friend "rot." In the real world, every decision has tentacles that reach into other decisions. The "right" answer depends on seventeen variables you won't know about until after you've acted. And sometimes – this is the part they don't tell you in those airport leadership books – sometimes there is no right answer. Sometimes you're just choosing between different flavors of imperfection.

Continuous Journey vs. Quick Fixes

You're not always going to get it right. You might just learn more from the mistake.

We're all addicted to the quick fix. Come on, admit it. You've bought the book that promised to make you a better leader in 21 days. You've attended the workshop that guaranteed transformation by lunch. Heck, I have a shelf full of them – "Leadership Secrets of [Insert Historical Figure]" and "The One Thing That Will Change Everything."

But you want to know a secret? The people writing those books know it's nonsense too. They know that real growth – the kind that actually sticks, that actually changes how you show up in the world – happens so slowly you barely notice it. It's like watching your kids grow. You don't see it day to day, and then suddenly they're asking for the car keys.

I used to think I was a slow learner. Why did it take me three years to finally understand what my mentor meant about "leading from behind?" Why did I have to make the same mistake four times before I got it? Then I realized: I wasn't slow. Life was just doing what life does – throwing new variations at me just when I thought I had it figured out. Think about it this way: You finally learn how to have difficult conversations with your team. Great! Then you get promoted, and suddenly you're having different difficult conversations with different people about different things. Ugh. That skill you developed? It helps, sure, but it's not one size fits all, nor does it work every time. It's more like... you learned French, and now you're in Quebec. Some words work, some don't, and sometimes you accidentally order sheep's brain when what you really meant was to ask for the bathroom.

The continuous journey isn't a bug – it's a feature. Every time you think you've arrived, the universe helpfully moves the finish line. Not because it's cruel, but because that's what keeps us alive, engaged, curious. The day you think you've got leadership all figured out is the day you should probably retire. Remember that highway metaphor I mentioned earlier? Scratch that. It's more like sailing. You can get better at reading the wind, trimming the sails, and navigating by the stars. But the ocean? The ocean doesn't care about your certificates or your years of experience. It's going to do what it's going to do, and you're going to keep learning, one wave at a time.

And honestly? Once you accept that – once you really embrace the idea that you're never going to be "done" learning how to lead – it is liberating. You can stop pretending you have all the answers. You can make mistakes. You can be curious instead of certain. The journey is continuous. Thank God. How boring would it be if we ever actually arrived? Remember when I said this isn't a roadmap? That's because roads end somewhere. It's like the sailing metaphor – you're always adjusting to the wind, and the horizon keeps moving. But that's not a bug in the system. That's the whole point.

CHAPTER TWO

The Learning Leader

Trisha Beck

From co-author to co-author

It's the quiet, observant ones who are the deep thinkers — the ones who notice the little things and become your steadying force. Trisha didn't say much during our first two semesters of doctoral coursework, but once we landed in the same capstone cohort group, I knew I had found "my person" for the journey and beyond. As fellow Scorpios born just two days and some years apart, we share a love of strategic approaches, considerate communication, and selective socializing. Trisha has been my anchor and confidant since we were randomly paired in our doctoral capstone group, and now we are co-authors of this book and so much more. And if she thinks she can get away from me, she'd better think again.

-Denise Nelson Nash

Leadership isn't about having all of the answers but instead it is about asking better questions and creating a space for exploration.

The Questions

At first, I dreaded the questions. Many years ago, as a new leader, I had the good fortune to work for what would become the greatest mentor of my long career. The Chief Executive Officer was a pediatrician by specialty. As you would expect from anyone with this specialty, he was kind and caring by nature. However, his very high expectations made him somewhat intimidating, especially for me in my first leadership role.

About once a month, he would show up in my office. With each visit came the questions: "Why do we...?" "Why don't we...?" "Can we do this better or differently?" Always questions I couldn't answer. I would reluctantly respond, "I'm not sure."

After each departure, I would sit in silence, reflecting on the questions he had presented. Determined to find the answers and rise to the challenge, I set out on my learning journey. I looked for information, asked questions, and dug deeper. Eventually, when I discovered the responses, I was always excited to share what I'd learned with him.

These follow-up conversations were always celebratory. What I didn't realize then was that we weren't just celebrating the answers. We were celebrating something much bigger; my transformation to become a Learner.

Growing pains. Originating in the 1800s, this term was often used when referring to children having a growth spurt. The literal pain (thought to be) experienced by the child as they experience their body growing. But what if I said this childhood experience was simply preparing us for the lifelong sensation of growing pains? How is any of this different from what you experience as a leader in times of learning and growth? You know that feeling- a bit of discomfort and pain.

Groundhog Day

I am a leader; I must avoid disruption. If I don't, I am a troublemaker.

In a world full of chaos and crisis, consistency and repetition feel like safe harbors. The status quo provides us with a sense of comfort. We know what to expect, there are no surprises. But what is the cost of remaining unchanged in a world that never stops changing? At the surface, stagnation and boredom. Dig deeper and we discover something far more alarming, paralysis. While we avoid the discomfort of learning, our teams are disengaging. Our competitors are innovating and improving. Our customers and clients are finding solutions elsewhere.

Many leaders find themselves trapped, living the same day over and over again; what I will call the Groundhog Day Trap. This trap is an endless cycle of making safe decisions that lack vision, establishing and adhering to comfortable routines that prevent growth, embracing familiar and comfortable processes that are predictable but ineffective, and repeating strategies and approaches while somehow expecting different results. In our quest to avoid being troublemakers we become exactly what troubles our organizations, obstacles to growth and progress.

So, how do you break the cycle? The learning leader makes a different choice and takes an alternate approach. Instead of fearing disruption they become strategic disruptors. A strategic disruptor: the leader who leverages new knowledge to innovate and create meaningful change and impact.

How do you become a strategic disruptor?

Challenge the patterns even when it feels uncomfortable. Every organization needs established patterns to function and thrive. Policy, procedure, and process; the structure that maintains quality, safety, outcomes and mitigates risk for an organization. But what about those patterns within our organization that continue simply because it is the way we have always done it?

Ask the questions others may avoid. Have you ever found yourself not asking a question because you weren't sure you really wanted to hear the answer? Maybe you had an idea of what the answer would be. Or perhaps you knew the answer would "open Pandora's box" and complicate an already complicated situation. Every organization has elephants in the room, issues that most are aware of, but no one discusses because addressing them would be expensive, create political challenges, or simply messy. The strategic disruptor asks these questions anyway.

These questions will likely cause temporary complications surfacing problems that are easier to ignore than address. The learning leader knows these unasked questions do not disappear, instead they fester and loom. The learning leader understands that facing the complexity of the questions now will prevent crises later.

Replace the comfort of repetition. Mastering a process that is repetitive can feel productive. You have done it so many times, you know the steps and you have perfected the process. The learning leader, or the strategic disruptor recognizes this mastery of what is familiar can become a barrier to exploration and growth.

Rather than defaulting to their historical knowledge and learnings, the learning leader asks, "What could we learn if we tried something different?" They try new things and experiment with fresh perspectives. Most importantly, they challenge their own assumptions and the assumptions of those around them.

Embrace the growing pains. The learning leader recognizes the discomfort and reframes the sensation of the growing pains; the pains are indicative of expansion and growth. The discomfort of not having the answer is your expertise expanding. When a new responsibility feels overwhelming, that is your capacity growing. At each of these moments is the evolution of you and the evolution of your team and organization.

Organically, our response is to eliminate these growing pains. The learning leader leans into these moments sharing their uncertainty with their teams, modeling curiosity, and demonstrating that leadership isn't about having all of the answers but instead it is about asking better questions and creating a space for exploration.

72 Hours

March 2020. The world was shutting down, and our patients still needed care. I stood in front of my team on a Tuesday morning with a big goal: build a telehealth program. Launch it by Friday. Keep patients safe. Keep staff safe.

The problem? I had never built a telehealth program. None of us had. We had barely used video calls in our personal lives, let alone integrated them into clinical care delivery. And we needed to operationalize this, technology, workflows, privacy compliance, clinical protocols, and staff training in 72 hours.

Every instinct I had as a leader told me I should have a plan before walking into that room. I should project confidence. I should have answers. But I didn't. And pretending I did would have wasted the limited time we had.

So I told them the truth. "Here's what I know: Patients need care, and they can't come into our facilities safely right now. We have 72 hours to build something that has never existed here before. Here is what I don't know: how to do that. I have never done this. Most of you haven't either. We are going to make mistakes. I am relying on you to tell me what is not working so we can fix it."

The discomfort in the room was palpable. Leaders aren't supposed to say "I don't know." But I watched something shift in their faces, not panic, but focus. Permission. If I didn't have all the answers, they didn't need to pretend they did either.

"So here's what we're going to do. We are going to try things. Fast. Some will work. Some won't. We learn and adjust."

For 72 hours, we operated in constant uncertainty. We built the technology infrastructure while simultaneously creating the workflows. We trained staff on platforms we were still configuring. We wrote policies for scenarios we had never encountered. And I was honest about every moment of not knowing.

In our daily check-ins, I started each meeting the same way: "What went well yesterday?" "What failed yesterday? What did we learn?"

By Friday, we launched. It wasn't perfect. The consent process was clunky. Some technical glitches remained. Our workflows had gaps. But patients received care. Safely. And we had a foundation to improve from.

What I learned in those 72 hours: the growing pains of not knowing weren't obstacles to good leadership. They were the foundation of it. My discomfort with uncertainty, that feeling of standing in front of my team saying "I don't have this figured out" well that wasn't a weakness. That was honesty. And that honesty created space for the people who did have pieces of the answer to bring them forward without waiting for permission.

If I had pretended to know, if I had spent the first day trying to develop the "perfect plan" before engaging the team, if I had hidden my uncertainty behind confident directives, we would have failed. Not because the team wasn't capable, but because I would have been solving the wrong problems while the people with actual expertise waited for me to tell them what to do.

That telehealth program became one of our most critical services throughout the pandemic. We served thousands of patients. We refined it constantly, protocols, technology, and workflows based on what we learned from each visit, each success, each failure.

But the foundation wasn't the technology or the protocols. The foundation was built in that first meeting when I said "I don't know" and invited the team to figure it out together. The growing pains of that week, the discomfort of leading without certainty, the vulnerability of admitting gaps in knowledge, the fear of making mistakes in a crisis weren't obstacles. Those were the ingredients of breakthrough performance.

Leadership isn't about having all the answers. It's about creating the conditions where the people who have pieces of the answer feel safe bringing them forward. Sometimes that means standing in front of your team and saying the scariest words a leader can say: "I don't know. Let's figure it out together."

The Antique Leader

I am a leader; I know it all. If I don't, I am an amateur.

Each of us brings a unique skillset and knowledge base to the work we do as leaders. We bring an encyclopedia of experience; lessons learned, strategies tested, and victories earned. This accumulated wisdom is valuable and essential to our success as leaders. We tap into this knowledge to make decisions and guide our work.

But here is the trap. Leaders will hoard their aged knowledge like vintage wine often believing what produced success in the past will automatically guarantee success in the future. In fact, these leaders proudly display their collection of outdated strategies as if in a museum approaching today's challenges with yesterday's solutions, not recognizing the world has fundamentally shifted around them. They are experts in a world that no longer exists.

Here is the truth; admitting you don't know something does not make you an amateur. It makes you current. The amateurs are those functioning with expired expertise while the world changes around them. The learning leader understands and embraces; leadership isn't about knowing everything, instead it is about knowing how to learn anything. Just like the journey you are on; the accumulated knowledge of the leader is not the final destination. Instead, it is a launching pad for new discoveries.

Learning leaders replace the comfort of certainty with the energy of curiosity. They know when they stop learning, they stop leading. They admit gaps in knowledge, question assumptions, and understand yesterday's expertise can become tomorrow's liability.

Your experience matters. Your knowledge is valuable. But true learning leaders combine this knowledge with humility to keep learning and courage to admit the world has expanded beyond what they already know.

What separates learning leaders from antique leaders? Learning leaders see knowledge as a launching pad, a foundation for what they haven't learned yet. They believe expertise means knowing how to learn. While antique leaders curate the past, learning leaders architect the future.

The Fatal Flaw

I am a leader, I must have all of the answers all of the time. If I don't, I am not competent.

We have all experienced the crushing weight of believing we must have every answer and demonstrate constant competence. This trap, the unspoken message that uncertainty equals incompetence transforms learners into performers, from those who question to those who claim to know it all.

This fatal flaw masquerades as strength. Today's world rewards quick decisions and decisive action. Leaders who speak with authority and rarely appear confused are promoted. But what if these behaviors actually limit our leadership potential?

Learning leaders ask questions to expand their knowledge and their team's knowledge. Questions are the learning leader's secret weapon; they expand knowledge, reveal challenging assumptions, illuminate blind spots, and uncover possibilities. Asking questions isn't weakness; it's intellectual courage.

The Power of the Pause

The pause, the sacred place between the question and the answer. This is where brilliance is born; solutions are found, where the real reflection and learning happens. But what do most of us do? We rush to fill this space, perhaps feeling the awkwardness and sense of discomfort. What is the result? We are rushing to respond instead of pausing to consider. We fill the silence with noise instead of embracing the silence to learn and understand. But the learning leader fuels their energy with the uncertainty of the silence, understanding the questions deserve thoughtful consideration, not just a hasty response.

The Power of Exploration

Learning leaders recognize the best solutions often are found outside of our current understanding. These leaders find power in exploring unknown territories. They understand our knowledge is always incomplete and our first answer is often not our best answer. This requires a purposeful shift in how we see ourselves and our roles. Instead of being the person with all of the answers, we are the person willing to question, to learn, and to grow.

So how do you break the cycle? Competence is about knowing how to learn anything, not about knowing everything. Listen more, speak less. Explore more. Inquire more. Gather information before making decisions. Understand more before providing answers and solutions.

So, what separates the learning leader from the fatal flaw leader? Learning leaders embrace the discomfort of uncertainty. They recognize these growing pains are the expansion of their current knowledge and limitations. As a result, teams feel allowed to explore what they don't know, and innovation is driven by collective discovery. While the fatal flaw leader believes competence means having all of the answers, the learning leader believes competence means knowing how to learn everything.

The Code Blue

I am a leader; I must respond and react to situations immediately. If I don't, I am indecisive.

She didn't just preach the "open door" policy; she lived it. Her door stood wide open, a constant invitation that I, a nervous, inexperienced leader accepted far too often. I treated her office like an emergency room. Daily, sometimes hourly, I would rush in, dumping a laundry list of perceived disasters at her feet. She never rushed me. She would sit back, hands folded, and listen to my frantic list of things that needed to change right now.

When I finally paused for air, she would lean forward and ask the same grounding questions: "Is anything on fire? Is anyone dying?" I would sheepishly answer, "No." "Good," she would say, the tension leaving the room. "We have time to make the decisions that need to be made."

In those quiet moments, she taught me the most valuable lesson of my career: Perspective. I realized that I was treating every bump in the road like a cliff edge. By classifying solvable problems as "catastrophes," I was wasting energy on anxiety instead of focusing on solutions. Once I understood that very few things are truly "on fire," I gained the clarity that I needed to lead.

In the healthcare space a code blue is a medical emergency. Every second counts, immediate and succinct action can mean the difference between life and death. But what happens when leaders treat every situation as if it is a code blue? The leader becomes the organization's first responder, jumping into action before completely understanding what they are responding to. These leaders believe that hesitation equals weakness and any pause or delay in action equals indecision.

The speed of decision does not determine the leader's character. In fact, the inability to distinguish between crisis and complexity creates organizational chaos. Chaos disguised as decisive action. What it really is? Recklessly impulsive behavior creating an organizational culture where everything is urgent and a priority.

For this leader, motion is progress when in fact it is not. The code blue leader bases decision on incomplete information gathered in haste, emotional reactions, and a surface level understanding of problems. The result is solutions that address symptoms while the underlying and true problems continue to persist.

I want to be clear, there are situations that require an immediate or prompt response; safety issues, real crises, and time-sensitive problems. It is the learning leader that can identify and recognize the difference. The leader that places importance on the power of the pause. The leader that understands the power of the balcony view, looking at the situation holistically before responding.

How do you break the cycle? This isn't about becoming slower; it is about becoming smarter. It is about replacing the energy derived from the immediate reaction and response with the deeper satisfaction of an effective response. The learning leader truly understands often, the most decisive thing a leader can do is deciding to learn more before deciding what to do.

So, what separates the learning leader from the code blue leader? The learning leader understands that decisions are improved by learning and not by speed. They can differentiate the problem requiring an immediate response and the more complex opportunities that require an understanding before responding. The learning leader is strategically responsive rather than impulsively reactive. While the code blue leader believes that leadership means immediate reactions, the learning leader believes that leadership means strategic responses.

The Space Between

I still remember the weight of the silence in my office after the CEO would ask, "Why do we do it this way?" and I had to answer, "I don't know."

In those early days, that silence felt deafening. It felt like a failure. My "Code Blue" instinct screamed at me to fill the air with noise, to invent an answer, to prove that I was worthy of the title on my door. I wanted to be the "Antique Leader," pulling a dusty solution from the shelf just to stop the burning sensation of uncertainty. But looking back, I realize that silence wasn't a void. It was a gift.

My mentor wasn't asking those questions to expose my lack of knowledge; he was carving out space for my growth. He was teaching me the power of the space between.

The space between is that terrifying, sacred gap between the question and the answer. It is the pause between the crisis and the response. It is the moment you stand in front of your team during a global pandemic, with no plan and 72 hours on the clock, and choose to say, "I don't know, but we will figure it out."

Most leaders spend their entire careers trying to close this gap. We rush to fix, to answer, to solve, because the "Growing Pains" of sitting in the unknown feel too much like weakness. We treat silence like a flatline, something that needs to be resuscitated immediately.

But the learning leader understands that the space between is the only place where true leadership lives. If you fill every silence with your own voice, you leave no room for your team to speak. If you fill every problem with your own answer, you rob them of the struggle that produces wisdom.

Embracing this space requires a different kind of bravery. It is the courage to let the silence linger. It is the strength to withstand the pressure of the "Fatal Flaw" that says you must be perfect. It is the humility to admit that while you are the leader, you are also still the learner.

So, the next time the pressure mounts and the room turns to look at you, do not rush. Do not panic. Do not treat the moment like a fire to be extinguished. Breathe. Step into the space between. That discomfort you feel? That isn't the feeling of failing. That is the feeling of learning. That is the feeling of leading.

CHAPTER THREE

Listening to Learn

Denise Nelson Nash

The Sunday Morning Soulmate

Something greater than chance brought us together in the same NYU doctoral cohort. We started what we thought would be study sessions every Sunday morning for two years- but they became so much more. From the first meeting, I felt her presence. Denise has this way of filling a room, even a virtual one, not with volume but with brilliance. She is calm and intentional, funny and gracious, and when she speaks, everyone leans in. Every Sunday she would show up with her coffee, her curiosity, her energy inspiring us to be Learners even when the world expected us to be the experts. Denise made me braver simply by being herself: kind, steady, and deeply human. Denise, who I now call my "cohort soulmate," showed me that real strength doesn't need to be loud, that leadership can be both gentle and influential, and that the people who change your life most profoundly often do it with consistent, loving presence. When we decided to write this book together, I knew Denise's voice, thoughtful, generous, and undeniably present, had to be woven through every word, because she embodies the truth we are trying to teach: that who you are matters more than what you know.

-Trisha Beck

I'm listening to learn.

Denise's Learning Journey

"A vertical line is dignity. The horizontal line is peaceful. The obtuse angle is action. That's universal, it is primary." Janet Collins

You might be thinking right now, what does this quote have to do with the Trinity of Leadership, and who is Janet Collins? First, if you don't know who Janet Collins was, I urge you to look her up. Quick snapshot: Janet Collins, an African American ballerina, choreographer, and teacher, was the first Black prima ballerina to perform at the Metropolitan Opera in New York City. She was my college dance instructor and mentor. But to truly understand why her words have had such an impact on me and why they became the lens through which I see leadership itself, I need to take you back to where it all began. Back to a time before I knew Janet Collins' name, before I understood that the movements my small body was learning carried wisdom that would shape decades of leadership to come. Because sometimes we live the lessons long before we have language to name them.

Pollyanna Dance Studio in Los Angeles — a space where childhood restlessness could be transformed into something with form and purpose. I was four, maybe five, when my parents recognized what I couldn't yet: my energy needed direction, and my curiosity needed a vocabulary. Dance gave me both. Steps became words. Movements carried meaning. My little body learned to speak in ways language hadn't yet taught me. But something more profound was happening in those mirrored studios with wood barres. I was discovering that order could emerge from chaos, that imagination could be shaped without being tamed.

After several years of performing others' choreography, something shifted. I began to see dances before they existed, and I started creating movements on other bodies. And they followed. I didn't recognize this as leadership then; I thought I was just making dances. But what I was really learning was how to translate the invisible into the visible, how to invite others into a vision they couldn't yet see, how to guide without controlling. The dance studio became my first classroom in the art of collaboration, in the courage to create, and the humility to revise when the movement didn't match the music.

This love of dance and creating worlds through movement became the thread woven through college and my first graduate school, where I earned an MFA not just in technique but in bringing visions to life. The studios gave way to stages in California, New York, and Venezuela. Each space taught me something new about the delicate balance between trust and structure. All the while, I was learning to lead before I truly knew what leadership meant. I was already living Janet Collins' wisdom—learning through my body what I would later understand through her words.

While my days on stage are well in the past, Janet Collins' simple yet profound observations have stuck with me throughout my leadership journey. Second, her words embody all aspects of the trinity of leadership — learning, thinking, and tinkering — in particular, learning. Let's break it down together.

"A vertical line is dignity." In dance, this might refer to an upright posture, composure, presence, and authenticity. In leadership, it represents standing with and within your truth, unwavering values, and uncompromising ethical standards. There have been countless situations where I had a choice – the choice to react, respond, or root myself within my values and integrity. These were all learning moments. No doubt this is familiar to you. Choosing is a skill that takes practice and repetition, like the dancer who perfects a movement sequence. It takes confidence in your convictions and beliefs when leading. With time, your self-respect translates into respect earned from others. There is something mesmerizing about this part of the learning journey. The subtle shifts accumulate with time until you feel your rootedness in the absence of your self-questioning. You know who you are, what you have to offer, and are willing to share and be you. There is also the aspect of having the courage to admit 'I don't know' or 'I need to have a better understanding' or 'I was wrong.' This is part of the leadership journey of maintaining your ethical center while being humble enough to grow. This takes us to the horizontal.

"A horizontal line is peaceful "— calm, stable, and supportive. In dance, this might be stillness in the extension of an arm or leg, a partnered sequence or lift, or a floor position. In leadership, creating a space of equilibrium where collaboration is nurtured and supported can be motivating and stabilizing. This is often where reflection and thinking occur. Like the dancer who pauses in space in time during an extension or lift, the leader uses horizontal time to focus on the human element and the value of community and interpersonal relationships – thinking time, reflection time, learning time. Mary Parker Follett, known as the "mother of modern management," emphasized the importance of democratic organization and participatory leadership along with the value of community. She advanced the concept of "power with" as opposed to "power over." When importance is placed on collaboration, balance comes into play. Learning from each other becomes a "power with." Having the confidence and courage to invite ideas and opposing viewpoints is where collective stability can occur. It's an advanced concept where deep listening leads to learning. And then there's the obtuse angle.

An obtuse angle breaks the calm and reaches into an energized state where dynamic things occur. This is where tinkering and disruptive actions can lead to change-making and new directions. Like the dancer who accelerates the pace, interjects the unexpected, and alters the rhythm of movement, effective leadership needs movement and energy — the unexpected, the tinkering with concepts and ideas to innovate, challenge, and change. Learning can sometimes become uncomfortable. Learning together is powerful. Follett's value of a community-engaged approach does just that — old knowledge is disrupted to make room for new learnings and understandings. The energy of discovery can create dynamic change. It creates forward momentum.

These geometric metaphors, thanks to Janet Collins, are a lens into the learnings I share next.

"You seem quiet today," my colleague observed. I replied, "I›m listening to learn."

The Mentor Who Listened

As my leadership journey shifted from the stage to higher education program management and oversight, I carried those early lessons with me — the patience to learn from observation and the capacity to absorb that which comes from truly inhabiting space and quieting the mind to hear what is being said. One afternoon during a senior team huddle, the head of our division outlined upcoming changes. The room buzzed with the energy of questions forming and the collective impulse to assume a defensive posture. But something in me stilled. I recognized the moment required presence, not performance. I set aside my usual interactive mode to truly hear what was being conveyed. That's when my colleague leaned over, curious, and noticed I was quiet. This simple exchange signals a way to be present and embodies a journey of leadership in contrast to a performance of leadership. The willingness to observe, absorb, and set aside ego requires conscious choice, made repeatedly, to pay attention rather than just react, assume, or judge. This trio of observe, absorb, and set aside ego is a key aspect of learning and the leadership journey.

Like the storyteller in chapter one, who learned from Mr. Indecisive, the Emperor with no clothes, and the Egoist, I too discovered the difference between prototype leadership and journey-based leadership by experiencing both. The prototype leader focuses on having the right answers and looking competent. It's about maintaining an image. There is limited learning, and those around this type of leader are reduced to being doers. When learning is the focus, the journey-based leader embraces uncertainty and admits not knowing. This type of leader is fed by curiosity and discovery and empowers others around them, leading to a ripple effect.

I had the good fortune of having a journey-based leader as a mentor in my professional life. I intentionally refer to this person as a mentor and not a boss or supervisor. They modeled curiosity over certainty and invited the knowledge and wisdom of others into every conversation and the decision-making process. Their approach was focused on professional growth, rather than just task completion. They created a culture of learning, encouraging team members to be adaptive, innovative, and creative.

Here's an example of what this looked like in practice. My mentor's boss — a person who commanded rather than collaborated — decided one of my programs didn't fit the institution's mission. The boss was alone in this thinking, but the boss had the power to launch an investigation. The boss had become a persistent thorn and a steady drain of energy and morale. Just the thought of defending the program was exhausting.

My mentor could have directed me to take action or defend the program; instead, questions were asked to gain insights and create space for perspectives that might have otherwise remained hidden. This was the moment when I learned the value of asking questions. It's one of the most powerful things a leader can do.

Asking questions is empowering. It infuses clarity into situations as it compels answers. Often, especially early in my career, I wanted to display my knowledge through statements and showcase my "knowing." I mistakenly thought this would garner respect and empower me. This was my insecurity peering out of my shield. For the seasoned professional observing, it was probably amusing and amplified my "newness" to leadership. In actuality, this led to missed opportunities, relinquishing the ability to understand the motivations and perceptions of others - to reflect. Through the simple act of asking questions, layers are revealed, and power dynamics shift.

Having my work questioned struck deep — deeper than I wanted to admit. I was invested in the program and the people who poured their commitment and creativity into it; I was taking it personally. I turned to trusted colleagues, not only to vent but to process. They helped me see that this was all about the other person's need or desire to impose themselves into the scene. Once I relinquished my ego and ceased handing my power to the boss, I felt more competent and better able to participate in the evaluation.

What was clear from my mentor's approach was that inviting others into the conversation shifted the dynamic from conflict to collaboration. Questions such as "help me understand the program and how it connects to our mission" and "if this program was eliminated or changed significantly, what would be the impact?" led to reflection and discovery. In that moment, I realized my mentor chose to learn and discover rather than blindly comply with a thinly veiled directive.

The outcome was a learning approach that led to enhancements, not just the mere survival of the program. Misinformation was addressed through questions. Data dispelled myths. And puzzling together on what-ifs created space for compromise.

This was a lesson in approaching problems with curiosity rather than defensiveness. The strategic disruptor found their grounding by identifying the traps: Groundhog Day repetition, Antique leadership, the Fatal Flaw of needing all the answers, the Code Blue impulse to react without thinking. They discovered that growing pains aren't something to avoid but something to lean into. That discomfort signals expansion, not weakness.

I learned that when we listen to learn, rather than defend, our opponent can make our work more aligned, stronger, and inclusive. And the courage to be curious deepens future collaborations across a group and organization.

The Mystery of Readiness

Learning also requires a state of readiness. What does that look like for you? For some, listening to learn is like developing a subtle skill that becomes more natural and available with practice. It becomes a part of who you are, rather than something you must consciously create. So, how do we get there? What does that look like? What do you think creates those moments of openness? It could be a life-changing event, maturity, situational factors, or many other things. The mystery of readiness to learn and the mystery of moments of openness should be recognized and honored when they appear.

Not all learning stories are comfortable or positive. Ultimately, learning leads to change, understanding, choice, or a combination. Whether the experience was positive or difficult, we emerge from learning different from how we were before with new understandings and knowledge that can be integrated into the next chapters. One such learning occurred to me early on in my professional career.

I spent several years living and working internationally. Once the glamour of being an expat in another country wore off, I was confronted with the reality of navigating my day-to-day life in an unfamiliar cultural context and another language. Initially, I leaned on my

English-speaking acquaintances and used index cards with phrases to help me get by with essential survival vocabulary: ¿Habla inglés? Gracias. Perdon. ¿Dónde está _____? ¿Cuánto cuesta esto? No entiendo. Lo siento, no hablo español. But soon, it became evident that I would need to venture out of the cocoon I had built around myself and immerse myself in the unfamiliar.

Pause moment - I want you to think about cocoons you may have built around yourself that may have prevented you from learning. Did you build what you believed to be safety, or perhaps it was just comfort? Or maybe it was an attempt to control instead of embracing a time to learn? Okay, back to the story.

Where my learning journey first went a bit sideways was assuming similar was the same. "Similar" is a key word in this story. I miscalculated that similar equated to the same and approached my transition into my new life "knowing." This is one of the fundamental mistakes often made in the leadership journey – assuming knowledge. The confidence that comes from past experiences overlaid on the current context can blind us to what is before us. This was a moment when experience became a liability rather than an asset. Or perhaps, I should refer to it as arrogance - the act of thinking I knew more than I did.

Ironically, I entered a new environment knowing versus learning and assuming expertise and knowledge that I had not acquired. This was partially based on assumptions and partially due to leadership conditioning. This goes back to the prototype leader who focuses on having the answers, knowing and not questioning, and assuming a posture of control. At this point in my career, I had only experienced this type of leadership, and while I resisted parts of the model leader, I unconsciously adopted the historic leadership norms. There was a moment when this became apparent, resulting in my readiness to learn.

I was hired to help build a program and teach, but in the end, I was the student. I was 26, two years out of graduate school, and full of knowing. I had taught in two states before accepting the international offer. Teaching is the same regardless of context and students, right? You create a lesson plan, deliver it, manage the class space, assess student progress, and ensure a positive learning environment - you lead the class. Oh, how wrong I was and how much learning I had to do.

Once I became more proficient in my second language, I grew closer to a few of my students - they were all young adults. I was invited to the home of one of my students, which was a lengthy bus ride from where I was living and a walk up a steep hill through a maze of dwellings. Upon arrival at the bottom of the hill, I was greeted by community members who were anticipating my arrival - the American teacher. It was a bit of a celebratory greeting, which threw me off. I was just a teacher, or so I thought. At that moment, I was introduced to a culture within a culture.

I was not prepared for the informal settlement and dynamic environment. I assumed, incorrectly, that all my students lived in neighborhoods of high-rise apartment buildings or single-family homes. As I peered up from the bottom of the hill, I saw a massive, interconnected network of makeshift, colorful shapes. The warm, beaming faces that greeted me were there to guide me through the labyrinth to my student's home.

Making my way up the hill through the passages created by the structures, I was curious and a bit apprehensive. I had only read about or seen these types of communities in the media, and it was always within a negative context. What was before me was a "Basquiat" neighborhood - full of symbolism, vibrancy, rejection, and hope. I turned off judgment and expectation and opened myself to learning. The act of ascending guided by the welcome committee was one of the most profound lessons in learning. I was the teacher being taught through acts of kindness, acceptance, appreciation, and genuineness. In that moment, the clarity of "similar" wasn't "same" came into full focus.

The moment of "similar" wasn't "same" wasn't really a moment, it was more of a gradual shift of recognition and realization. It was then that my leadership learning journey accelerated. Living internationally within another culture required me to observe, adapt, and learn constantly. I was keenly aware of my insertion into an unfamiliar space, but the shift required a multi-year period of learning to find comfort within another culture. It was also a time to let go of assumptions and allow curiosity to lead to discovery. It wasn't the first or last of my learning journey, but it was certainly one of the most profound.

Letting Go to Learn

This is going to seem like a left turn, but stick with me. A book that I have read dozens of times is The Alchemist by Paulo Coelho. It was years later, after my international learning journey, when I discovered Santiago's story, and I recognized my own journey in his. The Alchemist is the story of a shepherd boy who goes in search of a treasure and his own Personal Legend. I took some time to reflect on why this book resonates so deeply with me. In recounting my personal leadership learning journey, it became so clear and so obvious. The protagonist, Santiago, embarks on a journey that leads to letting go of his assumptions, recognizing that they were limiting his ability to learn and discover. The mentor figures in the story guide him through questions rather than direct answers, and in the end, he trusts his own wisdom to emerge. What he discovers is that the treasure was within him, but could only be found through the journey. This was exactly what my mentor had shown me in that exhausting battle over my program—that when I stopped giving my power away to defend my ego, when I let questions guide me instead of frustration paralyzing me, I discovered a competence that I had all along. The treasure wasn't in winning the argument. It was in learning to ask better questions.

The process of letting go requires curiosity. Curiosity is a gateway to letting go. For Santiago, it was his curiosity about his dreams, omens, and his willingness to wonder, "What if this is true?" This is at the heart of journey-based leadership and ties back to the quote, "I am listening to learn." This is inherently about curiosity and openness. The readiness to learn requires openness to receive and see. Receive new and different ideas. See what is around you through a fresh lens. Challenging certainties or assumptions – asking, "What if this is true?" Throughout my years in leadership, my readiness to learn fluctuated and was often situational. It took intentionality and awareness to develop consistency. To quiet the knowing mind and listen with curiosity and resist the expectation or pressure to have answers. Like Santiago, it has taken repeated encounters with the truth of not knowing to advance and grow.

Final thought: Be open and receptive to recognizing and honoring the natural rhythms of growth, rather than pushing against them - gift this to yourself.

PART TWO

THE THINKER

CHAPTER FOUR

Creating Space for Thought

Trisha Beck

*The Learner asks questions. The Thinker creates
space for those questions to breathe.*

In healthcare, we practice for what we can anticipate. We run drills. We follow clinical pathways, algorithms designed so nurses and doctors do the same thing every time. The goal makes sense: improve patient quality and safety by eliminating variation, reducing error, minimizing the need to think. If we can just minimize the human element, we minimize the risk.

But here's the irony, the very structures designed to protect patients can also prevent the thinking that saves them. What happens when the patient in front of you doesn't match the algorithm? When the standard protocol fails? When the emergency isn't the one you practiced for? That's when thinking matters most and when we are least prepared to do it.

This chapter is about breaking out of the rigidity that our structures impose. About creating conditions, in ourselves, in our teams, in our organizations where thinking isn't a luxury we can't afford, but the practice that makes everything else work.

Thinking happens in the spaces we create; in silence, in sanctuary, in sound, and in collaboration. Space to pause. Space to question. Space to think before we act, to reflect after we act, to think together instead of in silos. The Thinker's job is to create those spaces.

Not because we have all the answers. But because we understand that the best answers emerge from the culture we create, a culture where silence is comfortable, where sanctuary is protected, where thinking out loud is welcomed, and where collaborative problem-solving becomes how we work, not what we add to our work.

So how do we become the Thinkers we need to be? How do we create spaces that encourage individual and team thinking? How do we embrace the comfort of hearing our thoughts out loud?

Comfort in the Quiet

The Learner taught us that discomfort signals growth. The growing pains we feel? That is expansion, not weakness. The uncertainty we experience? That is learning, not incompetence. The Thinker takes that discomfort and transforms it into something productive; space. The learning leader asks questions. The thinking leader creates space to answer them. Space to not know yet. Space to sit with the question before rushing to the answer. Space to let the details reveal themselves before they try to solve the problem.

This is new territory for many of us. We are trained to act, to respond, to have answers. In healthcare, decisiveness can save lives. But decisiveness without thinking? That creates different risks. Here is the truth, comfort in the quiet means unlearning the urgency that says thinking equals delay.

Before we can create thinking space for others, we have to become comfortable in our own minds, comfortable with our own thoughts. Do you trust your own thinking? Or do you immediately second-guess, seek validation, defer to louder voices? Here is what I have learned, you can't invite others into a thinking space if you are not comfortable there yourself.

This isn't about being certain. It's about being comfortable with uncertainty. It's about building what I call an internal sanctuary, the ability to be present with your own thoughts without judgment, performance, or the immediate need to share or act.

Silence as Invitation

Here is what most leaders miss, your silence creates space for others to think. When you pause instead of immediately responding, you send a message. The message? There is room here for thought. When you resist filling every gap in the conversation, you invite others in. When you sit comfortably in the not-knowing, you give permission for others to do the same. It is your comfort with silence that gives others permission to think. Silence isn't empty. In fact, the silence is full of possibility.

Think about team huddles. Often, the leader asks "Any concerns?" and immediately moves on when met with silence. But what if you held that silence for ten seconds? Fifteen? Twenty? At first, it's uncomfortable. Eyes dart. People shift. But consistently, I have watched important information emerge from that silent space. The nurse who noticed a subtle change in the patient's condition. The assistant who had a question but didn't want to appear inexperienced. The pharmacist who caught a potential interaction.

How you hold the silence matters more than you might think. Your body language signals whether the silence is truly an invitation or just awkward dead air. I learned this the hard way in my early leadership roles, where my own discomfort, crossed arms, glancing at my watch, communicated impatience rather than openness. The team could feel me willing them to speak faster or, worse, willing the silence to end.

Now I approach silence differently. I keep my posture open: arms uncrossed, shoulders relaxed, body oriented toward the team. I maintain a neutral, slightly curious expression, not stern, not anxious, just present. I might nod slowly, as if giving people permission to think. Sometimes I look around the room making brief, gentle eye contact, not staring anyone down but acknowledging their presence. If I'm sitting, I lean slightly forward. If I am standing, I stay still rather than pacing or fidgeting. The message my body sends is: I have nowhere else to be. This space is yours.

Naming the silence beforehand helps tremendously, especially when you're first building this practice with a team. Instead of asking

"Any concerns?" and hoping someone speaks, try: "I am wondering if anyone has concerns or questions. Let's take 30 seconds together to think about it. If something comes to mind during that time, feel free to jump in." This simple framing transforms awkward silence into intentional reflection. The team understands they're not fumbling for words; they are being given space to process.

I have also learned to extend the silence after the first person speaks. Someone raises a concern, you address it, and then resist the urge to move on. Hold the space again. "Anything else?" And wait. Often the second or third person to speak offers the most critical insight, but they needed to see that it was safe, that you truly meant it when you asked.

The twenty-second pause feels eternal the first few times you try it. I remember counting silently in my head during an early morning huddle, convinced everyone could hear my heart racing. But around second twelve, a nurse spoke up about a patient's decreasing urine output, subtle enough that it wasn't alarming yet, significant enough that it changed our care plan. That intervention likely prevented a complication. It certainly wouldn't have surfaced if I had rushed past the silence.

Over time, your team learns that your silences are productive, not punitive. They begin to expect them. And as people become comfortable with the silence, they often speak sooner. But even when they don't, the silence itself communicates something essential: your thoughts matter enough for me to wait.

Make Your Thoughts Visible to Others

The Learner taught us "I'm listening to learn." The Thinker adds: "I'm thinking out loud."

Not all thinking is quiet. Some of the best thinking happens when we speak ideas into existence. When we articulate half-formed thoughts to see what they become. When we think out loud with others who help us see what we can't see alone. Do you have a thought partner who you invite to join your thinking? Does your thought partner give you permission to explore incomplete ideas?

But be cautious, thinking out loud requires self-awareness. Are you processing or performing? Are you inviting collaboration or dominating the space? Are you making your thinking visible or just making noise?

I learned this the hard way in a team meeting. I was thinking through a complex discharge plan out loud, or so I thought. What I was actually doing was performing my expertise, talking through my solution, not inviting others' thinking. The social worker finally interrupted: "Are you asking for input or telling us the plan?" That moment changed how I think out loud. Now I frame it, "I am processing this, can you help me think it through?"

Thinking in Motion: A Dance, not a March

Have you ever watched a Jack and Jill swing dance competition? The dancers meet at the edge of the floor and often they've never danced together before. The music starts, a song neither has heard in advance. And then they dance.

There is no choreography. No predetermined or practiced sequence of moves. Instead, the leader offers a suggestion through subtle pressure. A hand on the back, a shift in weight. The follower responds, adding their own interpretation, their own style. The leader feels that response and adjusts the next move accordingly. Back and forth, sensing and responding, creating something neither could have planned alone. Every dance is unrepeatable because every partnership, every song, every moment is unique.

Now compare that to a marching band. Precision. Synchronization. Every step mapped out weeks in advance. Everyone is moving in lockstep, following the drum major's lead without deviation. It's impressive but there is no room for adaptation. If something changes, the whole formation falls apart.

Thinking is a dance, not a march. It responds to what emerges. It adapts to new information. It partners with others' insights. It allows for improvisation within the structure.

In healthcare, marching looks like following the protocol regardless of what the patient in front of you needs. Dancing looks like using the protocol as your foundation, or your basic steps then adapting to this patient, this situation, this team's collective wisdom. The protocol tells you where to start. Your thinking tells you where to go.

The march prioritizes certainty and control. The dance prioritizes responsiveness and adaptation. Both have their place. A code blue requires marching. Everyone knows their role, no time for deliberation. But complex situations require dancing. Sensing changes, responding to what emerges, adjusting in real-time based on what the situation is telling you.

The Thinker knows which is which. More importantly, the Thinker knows how to shift between them.

Physical Movement Leads to Mental Movement

Here's something most people don't realize, your body affects your thinking. Sitting still in the same chair staring at the same screen often produces the same thoughts. Moving your body, walking, pacing, changing locations, unlocks new mental pathways.

There's neuroscience behind this. Movement increases blood flow to the brain. Changes in an environment trigger new neural connections. Physical shifts enable mental shifts. The Thinker uses this strategically. Scheduling walking meetings or standing meetings to energize the thinking process. Pacing while problem-solving. Actively changing locations when they are stuck. The Thinker knows movement creates momentum both physically and mentally.

Thinking Sanctuary

If comfort in the quiet is internal, sanctuary is external, the actual spaces and places where thinking happens. Where do you go to think? Not where you go to check emails, return calls, or complete tasks. Where do you go when you need to actually think? For me, it›s during early morning hours in my office before the day begins. The drive home at the end of a long day. The corner office with the door closed and my phone face-down. These spaces are different from the "doing" spaces, the spaces with constant interruptions, meetings, typically where the work is getting done.

What happens when the sanctuary is not available? This is where the Thinker's comfort in the quiet becomes portable. Intentionally creating a pause between reaction and response. Taking a breath before entering a meeting, the 60-second pause between responding to emails, or the conscious choice to pause before speaking.

Creating Sanctuary for Teams

Individual thinking matters. But the Thinker understands the importance of collective thinking. How do we intentionally create spaces that foster collective thinking?

Think about your typical meeting. Is it a thinking meeting or a "reporting" meeting? Someone shares information. Others half-listen while checking phones. Questions are asked. Decisions are made or deferred. Everyone leaves having heard information, but no one leaves having thought together. This isn't collaborative thinking. This is simply information sharing.

Let's begin with the physical space. Have you ever walked into a meeting and knew immediately if your role was to listen or to speak? The room setup determines thinking quality more than we realize. Consider a lecture hall where you go to receive information compared to the physical space with a circle or U-shaped design that signals the expectation of thinking and participation.

Now consider the same meeting. What does the agenda look like? Is there time for thinking clearly defined? I would guess the answer is no. Here is where structure beats spontaneity. "Feather in" thinking time, silent individual reflection time, thought partner time, or small group time. What does this accomplish? All voices contribute, not only the vocal ones and thinking happens at each layer within the team.

Other ways to create a thinking sanctuary and invite thinking for your team?

- Frame the question and not the answer
- Hold the silence. Some of the best insights may come from the person who needed 20 seconds to formulate their thought
- Make thinking visible. People can see connections and patterns and build on each other's ideas
- Protect the space. Interruptions derail thinking

Dolphin-Thinking

The most complex problems can't be solved by one person thinking alone. They require collective intelligence. But collective thinking is hard.

It requires structure, trust, and the willingness to think as a team, not just report individual thoughts to each other.

Imagine dolphins hunting. Why dolphins? Dolphins don't hunt alone. They use sophisticated communication, clicks, and whistles to coordinate in real time. Each dolphin contributes to the pod's intelligence. They are playful yet strategic. They adapt to what's happening, not what they planned would happen.

This is dolphin-thinking, collaborative problem-solving with constant communication. The metaphor captures what collaborative thinking requires: communication; bouncing ideas off each other to navigate complexity, constant, real-time, and adaptive; and cooperation: everyone contributes and the pod is smarter than any individual.

Magic happens when all that knowledge thinks together. Thinking Is a Team Sport Individual expertise matters. Collective wisdom matters more. The attending physician knows medicine. The nurse knows the patient. The pharmacist knows drug interactions. The social worker knows the family system. The patient knows their own body and life. That's dolphin-thinking.

Let's be clear, dolphin-thinking is NOT groupthink. Groupthink is when everyone agrees too quickly. The loudest voice wins. False consensus. Dolphin-thinking is often an active disagreement. Diverse perspectives invited. Quieter voices are drawn out. Genuine collaboration.

The difference is in the conditions and culture you create. Instead of the leader speaking first, the individual thinking comes first. Disagreement is expected and embraced. Pauses are intentionally created. Differences of thought are celebrated.

How do you know the difference? After your next meeting, do people leave aligned because they genuinely thought together? Or aligned because they didn't feel safe to disagree? It is thinking together where true alignment is found. The Thinker knows we are better together than alone.

From Thinking to Doing

Here is the challenge every Thinker faces; how much thinking is enough? Too little thinking, and you act prematurely perhaps solving the wrong problem, missing important information, creating new problems. Too much thinking, and you never act; analysis paralysis, hiding behind endless pontification of ideas, thinking as avoidance.

The Thinker navigates this tension and can identify the difference between productive thinking and overthinking. Productive thinking reveals new information, leads to clearer questions, moves closer to a decision, involves others when needed, and has an end point. Overthinking circles the same thoughts, creates confusion, avoids the decision, and has no end point.

The 70% Rule

Military leaders use the 70% rule: If you have 70% of the information you think you need, and you have used 70% of the time available, make the decision. Waiting for 100% certainty means the moment has passed.

In healthcare, waiting for absolute certainty often means waiting too long. The patient doesn't have time for your perfect answer. When you catch yourself thinking "I just need a little more information," ask yourself honestly: Will that information change my decision? If you can't articulate what specific information would alter your course of action, you already have enough to decide.

Decision Triggers

The Thinker sets decision triggers in advance. Before starting analysis, ask: What information would be sufficient to make this decision? What would need to be true for me to move forward? When you hit that threshold, you act even if you could gather more data.

In a patient deterioration scenario, I don't need perfect information about the underlying cause to start treatment. My trigger is: vital signs unstable plus two clinical indicators pointing in the same direction equals initiate intervention while continuing to gather data. The trigger removes the temptation to wait for one more lab, one more assessment, or one more consult before acting.

Your Thinking Partner

When you suspect you're overthinking, bring in a colleague. Not to make the decision for you, but to help you see whether you have enough to decide. Tell them: "I have been working on this decision for [time period]. Here is what I know. Here is what I'm wrestling with. Do I have enough to decide, or is there something I am genuinely missing?"

Often, explaining your thinking out loud reveals you already know what to do. The act of articulating the decision to another person clarifies what was murky in your own mind. Sometimes they will identify a genuine gap: "Have you considered...?" More often, they will reflect back: "It sounds like you have already decided."

Set a rule for yourself: If I have been thinking about this decision for X hours without progress, I consult someone. Fresh eyes cut through the mental loops you have been running.

What Overthinking Feels Like

Your body knows before your mind does. Learn to recognize the physical sensation of overthinking versus productive thinking.

Overthinking (analysis paralysis) feels like mental spinning, circular thoughts, physical tension, decision fatigue. I notice my shoulders creeping toward my ears. I am rereading the same information for the third time without absorbing anything new. My jaw is clenched. That's my body telling me I have crossed from thinking into avoidance.

Productive thinking feels like movement, new connections forming, questions becoming clearer, energy building toward resolution. There is a quality of momentum even when I am sitting still.

When you notice the physical signs of overthinking, that is your cue. You have extracted all the value thinking will provide. Now you need action to generate new information. Stand up. Make the call. Write the email. Start the conversation. Let your body break the mental loop.

Sometimes the best way to think is to do. Small actions generate information that thinking alone cannot produce. Instead of endlessly deliberating about a new workflow, pilot it with one team for one week. The data from that experiment will tell you more than another month of meetings.

The Thinker knows when to stop thinking and start doing. More importantly, the Thinker knows that doing and thinking aren't opposites, they are partners in a cycle of continuous learning.

The Rhythm of Thinking Leadership

The Thinker doesn't think once and act. The Thinker has a rhythm: Think → Act → Reflect → Think → Act → Reflect

Not think forever, then act. Not act without thinking. But a continuous dance between thought and action. This is where the Thinker becomes the Tinkerer.

The Learner asks the questions. The Thinker creates space for those questions. The Tinkerer experiments with answers.

Creating the Conditions

You don't control whether people think. You can create the conditions where thinking can happen. You create conditions through silence, sanctuary, sound, and collaboration.

- Silence: Pausing long enough for thoughts to form
- Sanctuary: Protecting time and space for thinking
- Sound: Making thinking visible and collaborative
- Collaboration: Thinking together as dolphins, not alone in towers

The Thinker's job isn't to have all the answers. It is to create the spaces where answers can emerge. During the silence when we're brave enough to sit in the not-knowing. In sanctuary, when we protect thinking from the tyranny of urgency. In sound, when we think out loud and make our thoughts visible. In collaboration, when we think together, we are adaptive, communicative, and constantly learning.

The Algorithm Can't Think

Remember where we started? The healthcare structures designed to minimize thinking?

Here's what the Thinker knows, protocols and pathways are necessary. And thinking is necessary. The art is knowing when to follow the algorithm and when to think beyond it. When the patient matches the protocol, follow it. When something feels off, pause and think. When the team sees something different, create space to think together. When the outcome isn't what you expected, reflect and learn. This isn't slower. It's smarter.

CHAPTER FIVE

Cultivating Conditions for Thought

Sharon Counts

The Chance Encounter

Of all the places to meet someone, I encountered Sharon at the Louvre Abu Dhabi, standing in the newest exhibit. There she was with a calm, grounded energy approaching me with genuine warmth. We started talking, and within minutes it felt like we had known each other for years. There is something about meeting someone in a place of beauty, surrounded by art and creativity, that strips away the usual small talk. We connected instantly over more than just the display before us. Sharon had this calm presence, yet was a creative force, and I could feel it even in that first conversation. What I didn't know then was that this person I had met by chance in Abu Dhabi would become part of my Circle of Trust, that she would become part of the very book we are writing. Meeting Sharon at the Louvre wasn't just a pleasant museum moment, it was being placed with the right person in my path at the right moment.

-Trisha Beck

Survival of the Thinker depends on leaders who make thinking about the work as important as the work itself.

Strong and Wrong

There are some things you only learn when everyone is watching—and apparently, mine involve choreography and bright red pants.

The first was in college, during a workshop with the renowned Pilobolus Dance Company, famous for highly athletic, imaginative modern dance that pushes the limits of human physicality. Paired with a 6'3" partner, towering over my 5'5" frame, to work on weight transference. I tried to lift him, to shift his weight, but my timing was all wrong. My muscles tensed, my heart raced, and every failed attempt made me feel smaller and clumsier than I already did. Suddenly, the facilitator's voice cut through the music: "Girl in the red sweats—just stop!" Frozen, cheeks burning, acutely aware of every eye on me, feeling like I had failed in front of the gods of modern dance.

Years later, the red pants reappeared in a very different setting. As the Director of Education and Community Engagement at New York City Center staff were invited to perform in a revue-style show called *Jamboree!*. We were asked to perform two numbers from *A Chorus Line*, a show I adored but had no business attempting. First came the high-energy opening number, followed by the show-stopping, precision-heavy number One. We had only one brief rehearsal on stage for this production, which was directed by Tony Award-winner Michael Mayer and featured Broadway stars Sutton Foster and Jonathan Groff. Being on that stage felt like standing on the edge of a cliff with no safety net.

The synchronized choreography of One demanded a level of precision I didn't possess. Inevitably, I made a mistake—one that couldn't be hidden. Standing frozen under the blinding stage lights, mortified, I heard Michael Mayer's voice over the God mic: "Girl in the red pants, you are not doing the right choreography." My stomach sank. Every muscle stiffened. The room felt impossibly large. Then, cutting through the tension, Jeanine Tesori—the most prolific and honored female composer in Broadway history, who was producing the show—used her own God mic and said: "She has a name—it's Sharon Counts."

The unexpected validation hit like a wave, especially because I was certain I was about to get fired. A smile crept across my face, relief flooding through the humiliation. My dancing was far from perfect, but I was seen. Fully. Mistakes and all. Red pants, it seemed, had become an odd, recurring badge of courage—a reminder that even in the spotlight, with all eyes on me, I could keep moving, keep learning, and even find joy in the chaos.

In the performing arts, strong and wrong is an expression about how performers fully commit to choices they make on stage, meaning how they express the intention of a gesture, movement, or word. A performer's choices are the decisions they make to interpret a character, including their emotional reactions, physical behavior, and how they deliver lines of dialogue. These choices are how an actor brings a character to life, making them specific and unique, and are based on their understanding of the character's objectives, obstacles, and motivations. A performer won't know how their choice reads until the director or choreographer reflects back on how it landed after experiencing the performer's choice. Sometimes the full commitment of the choice is what makes it believable, and sometimes it falls flat. However, the commitment to the choice itself is what allows the performer to put an idea forward. A rehearsal room is a perfect laboratory for experimentation. In that context, a performer has agency to think in draft and to make bold choices, strong and wrong.

What if our workplaces operated more like rehearsal rooms? This would allow the Thinker to float an idea to see how it lands, and to experiment without the consequences of outcome bias. A thinking environment mirrors that of a rehearsal room, where there is a commitment to the ongoing exploration and development of possibilities and ideas. Here, the Thinker can be productively brave and can put an idea forward or elevate a hypothesis that is untested. In this environment, experimentation is celebrated, and the process itself is rewarding. A thinking environment, like that of a rehearsal space, has a clear commitment to ongoing experimentation and is a space where there is iteration and evolution. In this space, it is safe to make bold choices, to take big swings, and to ideate without judgment, strong and wrong.

Strong and Wrong is about courageous iteration, it's a part of how the Thinker moves within a thinking space. How the Thinker begins, how we enter into a thinking space and strong and wrong is about how we act once we're inside it. When there is belonging, we can take risks and when there is celebration, we value the process. Strong and Wrong turns thinking into a performative and communal act where the Thinker can commit boldly to ideas without fear of being wrong, just like a rehearsal space. In this thinking space we are not seeking perfection, but shared experimentation. This is a place where ideas can be tested without shame. Reflection, such as a director's feedback, becomes a part of the learning, and mistakes are not errors, but are iterations of thought.

The Thinker's journey begins with belonging and celebration with the understanding that how we welcome ourselves and others into the act of thinking shapes everything that follows. Beginning is not just a starting point; it is a condition we cultivate. It's how we create the circumstances that allow curiosity, trust, and imagination to emerge. Strong and Wrong continues that journey. It reminds us that once we're inside the thinking space, courage becomes our method. Thinking, like rehearsal, is an act of presence and commitment. We test ideas not to prove them right, but to see what they reveal. We experiment, we revise, we begin again. In this process, belonging offers safety, and celebration transforms effort into energy. These ideas form the rhythm of the Thinker's practice: to enter with openness, to stay brave, and to keep thought in motion. The Thinker knows that to begin is to be brave, and to be brave is to begin again, strong and wrong.

Dark weeks are rare: the theater closes, performances stop, and no work occurs. Stephanie Ybarra led Baltimore Center Stage as Artistic Director from 2018–2023, making staff well-being a priority. Together with her team, she created the *Big Think*, a radical practice that carved out two full dark weeks in the production calendar—one for rest, and one for collective ideation. After a week of rest, the second week dedicated to the *Big Think* operated differently. Hierarchies were suspended; staff chose the topics, curated the agenda, and were encouraged to think boldly. Stephanie stepped back as a thought leader, creating a space where ideas could surface without fear of judgment.

The results were transformative. Staff felt truly seen and valued, and the organization generated innovative ideas that advanced its mission in unexpected ways. By structuring a space to be strong and wrong, Stephanie showed how intentional leadership can unlock creativity, collaboration, and new possibilities.

Cultivating Curiosity

Cultivating curiosity requires the Thinker to lead with integrity. Having integrity means that you can be quick to change your opinions but slow to change your principles. It takes openness to update your views and integrity to uphold your values. Listening cultivates curiosity, and the Thinker stokes it through empathy, patience, humility, and trust. Thinking happens most productively in spaces that are safe and brave, where ideation and exploration can occur without judgment and where listening is active and authentic. Foundational components include joy, curiosity, courage, generosity, and self-awareness. Cultivating curiosity also requires tolerating discomfort and leaving space for reflection.

Nourishing thinking requires skill and strategy. In theater, a director's job is to ensure the ensemble performs in the same show—that actors truly listen to each other rather than simply waiting for their cue. When performers aren't listening, dialogue feels stale and inauthentic. The same dynamic appears in workplaces when people listen only to speak, not to hear. A lack of curiosity functions like a closed mind: it shuts down the Thinker. When curiosity meets the adage "this is the way we've always done it," progress grinds to a stop. The Thinker thrives on cultures of open inquiry.

Stepping into leadership as a change maker can feel like being an understudy suddenly called into the lead role—expected to carry the weight of the production without rehearsal, while every choice is measured against what came before. The young girl waits in the wings for someone to say, "Hey kid, you're on," and arrives with wide-eyed eagerness, only to discover a room convinced the show has already been made.

This was my experience entering a senior role at a major performing arts institution. The environment seemed to lack curiosity. Questions meant as invitations to understand. *Why do we operate this way? Why is this system structured as it is?* —were received as challenges. Curiosity itself was treated as a disruption.

The Thinker's instinct is to ask why. But in organizations that treat questions as threats, even genuine curiosity registers as insubordination. The work continued—building community, strengthening collaborative relationships—but progress was slow. Some environments resist the Thinker's methods.

Clarity often comes with distance. Change always involves loss. To lead change is, in part, to ask others to give something up. Leading change is less like stepping into a starring role and more like asking a theater company to restage a show it has performed for years. Even small adjustments require effort, trust, and a willingness to release the familiar. In organizations that value product over process, curious questions can register as interruption. This is a structural challenge, not a personal failure.

Curiosity is the Thinker's way of staying awake to possibility. The Thinker thrives in spaces that are both safe and brave, where exploration can happen without judgment and where listening is active, authentic, and mutual. The Thinker cultivates curiosity through empathy, patience, humility, and trust—qualities that turn thinking into a relational act rather than a solitary one. Generosity and celebration also play a role: generosity opens pathways of connection, and celebration keeps the atmosphere joyful and expansive. Together, they create conditions where curiosity can take root and grow.

The Thinker expands learning and unlearning capacities to deepen awareness of areas for growth. Reflecting reveals what is meaningful and what fosters connection. Thinking into spaces where there is room to grow leads to productivity and confidence. Working collaboratively and individually requires building muscles around being together and listening together. This ecology turns thinking into a communal, ethical, and creative act- not only a cognitive act, but a fully human one. How we relate through trust and generosity and how we begin through curiosity are not just preconditions for thinking, they are thinking.

Cultivating curiosity deepens and extends the ideas of trust and generosity that anchor the thinking process. Just as belonging provides the psychological safety for thought to emerge, curiosity keeps that thought alive. To cultivate curiosity, the Thinker must lead with integrity, holding fast to core values while remaining open to new ideas and perspectives. This balance allows the Thinker to adapt thinking without compromising principle. Curiosity is not merely a trait but a discipline: a continual act of listening, questioning, and imagining that keeps both the self and the collective in a state of learning. For the Thinker, cultivating curiosity is a daily practice of renewal. It is how we begin and begin again. It is how we stay present, generous, and courageous. Curiosity keeps the Thinker in motion—learning, unlearning, and listening—so thought remains alive.

If You Can't Fix It, Feature It

The Thinker is unafraid of making mistakes or not knowing the answers. When we become secure in our own abilities and knowledge, it's much easier to let go of the need to be right or to be the smartest person in the room. Perhaps for me, a combination of age and experience has led to letting go of trying to have all the answers. In fact, I now delight in not knowing in some instances. I feel secure in my knowledge and no longer have the need for that to be all-encompassing. None of us is an expert in all things. The solid foundation of self-awareness that I have tended to and continue to work towards allows me to feel secure in not knowing all things. It's from this same place that I can acknowledge when I make mistakes.

As a theater director, I have often joked that I make rapid-fire decisions, strong and wrong. A leader who is a Thinker doesn't come to the table with all the answers. Instead, a Thinker can facilitate a process to cultivate curiosity and exploration around a shared purpose that will yield a variety of results. Not every offering in a thinking session will lead to the right answer, and sometimes, as much as and as hard as we think, we come up against resistance and roadblocks.

A colleague, friend, and former professor of mine in graduate school at New York University, Joe Salvatore, taught me an idiom that he applies to directing and teaching that can easily be applied to leadership, which is "If You Can't Fix it, Feature It." Sometimes in a production, there's a scene or a transition that just isn't coming together, and by leaning into the messiness of the moment, a director can invite the audience in to experience that moment in a new and authentic way. In the classroom, a student who seems to be distracted or is distracting others can be invited into a new role as an assistant or leader, which gives the student agency in their learning. The same thing can be true for a Thinker with the self-awareness and assuredness that allows them to make and acknowledge mistakes. That is not failure, that is strength. We all make mistakes, and to pretend otherwise is not only an affront to integrity but it is a demonstration of weakness and a lack of thinking.

We see so many examples of leaders who refuse to get out of the way; leaders who won't take responsibility, acknowledge the problem, or apologize for wrongdoings and mistakes. Making mistakes is human. Leaders are human beings, and there is no such thing as a human being who is infallible. There is no evolution or innovation without failure. Let's embrace the mess and celebrate the failures, even the ones that cut us deeply. I have failed spectacularly more than once on my leadership journey so far, and I have every reason to believe that I will continue to make mistakes, strong and wrong. To me, how a Thinker handles those failures or opportunities, depending on one's mindset, says more about who we are as leaders and people than whatever the mistake was.

If Strong and Wrong is about courage and Cultivating Curiosity is about openness, then If You Can't Fix It, Feature It is about acceptance—the Thinker's ability to embrace imperfection as part of the process and to let go. The Thinker is unafraid of mistakes or not knowing. When we are secure in our abilities and grounded in self-awareness, we can let go of the need to be right. That freedom makes room for exploration, humility, and growth.

In the rehearsal room, when a scene refuses to come together, a director might choose to lean into the imperfection-to feature it-inviting the audience to experience the moment honestly. The same is true for the Thinker. When we face resistance, uncertainty, or failure, we can choose to engage with it rather than conceal it. Featuring what feels broken transforms limitation into innovation and strengthens trust through authenticity. To feature what cannot be fixed is to stay curious, to model courage, and to remain human. The Thinker acts with bravery, builds with trust, cultivates curiosity, and continues to evolve through imperfections, with the understanding that the beauty of thinking lies not in getting it right, but in staying open to what the thinking reveals.

Celebration

Thinkers are often strategic problem solvers focused on the big picture. Celebration creates space to pause, reflect, and restore hope. It reinforces connection, collaboration, and culture by honoring not only outcomes, but the effort, risk, and learning that lead to them. When Thinkers model celebration—recognizing small wins, bold attempts, and even failures—they foster gratitude and community, creating conditions where curiosity, adaptability, and deep thinking can flourish.

Celebration is not just about success; it is about honoring effort, courage, and vulnerability. Working at *Blue Man Group* (BMG) was my first job after moving to New York City. I interviewed on my very first day in the city, having just arrived from Los Angeles. The people who made up that company became my artistic family and laid the foundation for my life in New York.

Through BMG, I joined the Broadway/Off-Broadway Softball League. Our team was strong, and we made it to the finals against the cast and crew of *The Producers*, who had won a record-breaking twelve Tony Awards that same year. The game was fun and fiercely competitive. In the end, Matthew Broderick made an incredible play that sealed their win.

Before the Producers team could even react, the BMG team erupted into an exuberant chant: *"We're number two! We're number two!"* Band members appeared with drums and hand instruments, and the field turned into an impromptu dance party. The Producers team stood stunned for a moment, then joined in, swept up by the unrestrained joy. In that moment, our celebration wasn't a denial of losing—it was a conscious choice to honor how we had shown up together.

On opening night of *Blue Man Group*, Chicago, the audience was filled with friends, family, and staff from New York and Boston who had flown in for the occasion. The Blue Man character—part shaman, part clown—explores the human condition through wonder, humor, and music. In rehearsals, performers use the classic red clown nose to develop the character, paradoxically revealing vulnerability and humanity rather than concealing it.

That night was especially meaningful: the three original creators of BMG, who had largely stopped performing, were onstage together. My boss, the Artistic Director, and I wanted to unite the audience in celebration while they performed. In the pre-internet era, we spent more than a week scouring Chicago to find 625 red clown noses—one for every audience member.

Midway through the show, the Blue Men gathered at the edge of the stage, shared a quiet check-in, and then raised their arms toward the audience in a gesture of openness. A burst of white light and percussive energy filled the theater, allowing performers and audience to truly see one another. In that exact moment, all 625 audience members put on their red noses.

The creators broke character, smiling and laughing as a spontaneous standing ovation erupted. We saw them, they saw us, and together we transformed an audience into a community through a shared experience. That moment reminded me that celebration is not an interruption of the work—it is part of the thinking itself.

Celebration validates process, not just outcomes. Recognizing small wins, experiments, and missteps reinforces the value of iteration and encourages ongoing curiosity. By celebrating attempts rather than only results, leaders reduce fear and judgment, creating psychological safety for Thinkers to experiment boldly.

In a thinking environment, celebration honors effort, builds connection, reinforces learning, and reduces fear of failure. It turns thinking into a shared, resilient, and joyful practice—one that expands what becomes possible.

Survival of the Thinker

Survival of the Thinker is not a standalone principle, but the outcome of a sustained thinking practice. For Thinkers, survival is not only about endurance—it is about maintaining the conditions that make thinking possible. Celebration is one of those conditions. In complex and ever-changing environments, the Thinker survives by using thinking itself as a form of resilience. They pause, reflect, and reframe problems, finding pathways forward when others cling to old solutions.

A Thinker's voice is not always the loudest one, or even the most knowledgeable one, but they are the most resilient one, due to cultivating an adaptability mindset. Survival depends on curiosity, openness, and the ability to synthesize new ideas, rewarding those who think critically, creatively, and strategically. Leaders who embrace this mindset make space for reflection, encourage exploration, and turn challenges into opportunities for learning and innovation.

Survival of the Thinker depends on leaders who make thinking about the work as important as the work itself. Central to this approach are four guiding principles: Strong and Wrong, Cultivating Curiosity, If You Can't Fix It, Feature It, and Celebration.

Strong and Wrong – Courage in Action

Survival begins with boldness. Strong and Wrong is about committing fully to a choice or idea, even if it might fail. Mistakes are not evidence of failure—they are opportunities for iteration and learning. In the theater, performers experiment with making choices, strong and wrong, to discover what works. In organizations, Thinkers apply the same mindset to test ideas, elevate hypotheses, and innovate without fear of judgment.

Belonging and celebration create a safe space for this experimentation. Just as rehearsal rooms allow performers to explore, test, and refine, a thinking environment allows Thinkers to act courageously, put forward bold ideas, and commit to exploration. Mistakes are iterations of thought, essential to growth.

Cultivating Curiosity – Openness and Engagement

Curiosity is the engine of thinking. The Thinker thrives in environments where listening is authentic, inquiry is encouraged, and assumptions are challenged. Cultivating curiosity requires integrity: being willing to revise ideas without compromising core values.

Curiosity is relational, not solitary. Through empathy, patience, humility, and generosity, Thinkers turn questioning into a communal act, where dialogue, exploration, and discovery become shared experiences. In leadership, curiosity helps uncover entrenched practices, invite new perspectives, and guide teams through change—just as performers must listen and respond to one another on stage.

If You Can't Fix It, Feature It – Acceptance and Adaptability

Not every problem can be solved, and not every situation can be controlled. The Thinker's strength lies in embracing imperfection and using it as a tool. If You Can't Fix It, Feature It is about leaning into the messy, the unresolved, and the unexpected, and turning it into opportunity.

In rehearsal and in classrooms, moments that seem broken can be highlighted, featured, or reframed to generate learning and connection. In leadership, this principle encourages letting go of the need to always be right, to see mistakes as moments for growth, and to allow others' agency to flourish. Accepting imperfection fuels resilience, innovation, and authenticity.

Celebration – Joy as a Strategic Practice

Thinking is not just about problem-solving—it's about engagement, presence, and energy. Celebration sustains resilience by acknowledging progress, effort, and courage. Whether it's a successful experiment, a breakthrough insight, or simply the act of showing up and thinking together, recognition reinforces belonging and motivates ongoing participation.

Celebration transforms effort into energy, mistakes into learning, and ideas into shared achievement. It is the rhythm that sustains the Thinker's practice: beginning with curiosity, acting with courage, accepting imperfection, and honoring the journey.

Together, these principles form a framework for survival and flourishing in complex environments. The Thinker begins with curiosity, acts boldly strong and wrong, navigates challenges by featuring what cannot be fixed, and sustains momentum through celebration. This approach creates a thinking ecosystem that is resilient, adaptive, and generative—where ideas, people, and leadership evolve together.

Survival of the Thinker is not about certainty or control. It is about creating the conditions that allow thinking to continue—especially when the path forward is unclear. When we lead with curiosity, act with courage, accept imperfection, and take time to celebrate, we build environments where thinking can stay alive. In those spaces, ideas are not rushed or silenced, people are not reduced to outcomes, and learning becomes a shared, sustaining act. This is how Thinkers endure—not by closing themselves off, but by remaining open to what emerges next.

CHAPTER SIX

The Power of Thinking

Herminio L. Perez

The Toothbrush

The first time I met Herminio, he handed me a toothbrush. Definitely an unusual way to greet someone at a first meeting. Let me provide some context.

It was the first day of our doctoral residency. Thirty cross-sector professionals had been brought together for what was promised to be a transformative experience, and none of us knew each other. We gathered in a boardroom with rows of seating on either side of the open center space for speakers. After the first session ended, the room buzzed, and we poured out of our seats to meet our new cohort members. We introduced ourselves by name, location, and sector. But in the midst of all the energetic conversation, a calm, kind face emerged in the group, moving toward me, holding a toothbrush. Herminio is a dentist and dental educator, so naturally, he introduced himself by handing me a toothbrush. It happened so quickly that I didn't have time to check my breath or my teeth for pieces of stray breakfast. His presence immediately put me at ease. He is the humanist of our author group—one of those rare individuals who brings out the best in each of us.

-Denise Nelson Nash

Happiness comes when you turn your knowledge into a resource.

"Where did your journey as a Thinker begin?" Someone recently asked me—a question that lingered in my mind long after the conversation ended. Looking back, I realize it wasn't a single moment or inspiration, but the twists and turns of my own personal and professional life that compelled me to become a relentless seeker of answers. The circumstances I faced and the experiences I lived through didn't just nudge me toward curiosity; they launched me into a lifelong quest to unravel every puzzle that life could throw my way. This relentless pursuit of solutions is where my story truly begins.

My upbringing played a significant role in shaping my approach to life, as did my faith and the absence of consistent guidance. I was also driven by the belief that education could provide all the answers I needed. This belief motivated me to explore every possible resource that could help me overcome life's challenges. This constant need to problem-solve led me to rely on books and my friends, who supported me in my quest for answers.

Faced with these limitations as a student with restricted financial resources, I asked myself a pivotal question: What could be more affordable, engaging, and illuminating than turning to books as a source of answers? (don't get me wrong, I really enjoy going to a bookstore and having a book in my hands and deciding which one to take with me). At that moment, an idea illuminated my mind. I realized that thinking itself was the answer.

Early in my career, I began working as a hospital dentist in the Bronx, New York—an environment that immediately felt like home. As a Puerto Rican surrounded by others from the diaspora, I took comfort in the rich tapestry of cultures within my community and among our Caribbean neighbors. Immersed in this world, I gained firsthand insight into their daily challenges: barriers to healthcare, limited access to education, and struggles with housing. Every patient's story and expression revealed the realities they faced, encouraging me to look beyond the dental chair and understand the broader context of their lives. I found myself asking: What can I truly contribute here? What is my purpose within this community? Why does serving this community matter so deeply to me? Through these experiences, I realized the profound power of thinking that comes from asking reflective questions. Each moment of self-inquiry helped me not only to empathize with those I served but also to deepen my own understanding and commitment to making a meaningful impact. These thoughtful reflections became a driving force in my journey, guiding my actions and shaping my purpose within the community.

Listening to their stories instilled in me a profound sense of purpose. Through these experiences, I discovered not only the reason behind dedicating a significant "chunk" of my life to dental care, but also the deeper meaning that connects oral health to overall well-being. Restoring the function of the mouth was just one aspect; far more rewarding was helping individuals reclaim the confidence to smile openly once more. In those moments, I truly understood how my knowledge could serve as a resource for good—restoring smiles and hope within the community I was honored to serve.

Each smile came with a "gracias," "thank you." Sometimes with some tasty recipe from our "homemade" Caribbean cuisine or some sweet pastries. Being able to relate to their needs and to look like them gave an extra point and a warm hug from each patient I served. For a decade, I was able to be part of a community that taught me to find the purpose and meaning of my profession.

Years later, I was given the chance to join an outreach program alongside a group of students. Although I was both nervous and excited, I welcomed the opportunity to use my knowledge and skills to serve those most in need. This time, our focus was on children and families living in the sugar cane fields of the Dominican Republic—a truly humbling experience. Their happiness and contentment, despite their limited resources, left a lasting impression on all of us. I watched children running freely through the fields with so little, while we often found ourselves lamenting what we lacked. Then, I found myself again asking: What can I truly contribute here? What is my purpose within this community? Why does serving this community matter so deeply to me?

One moment remains especially vivid in my memory: the day I handed a toothbrush to one of the children. His reaction caught me completely off guard. He stood perfectly still, eyes wide and brimming with tears, before wrapping me in a heartfelt embrace. When I gently asked why he was crying, he replied that no one had ever given him anything before, and he was deeply moved by this small act of kindness.

The sense of fulfillment and humanistic accomplishment was my true reward. Not only did I provide a compassionate experience for a group of students, but I also had the privilege of teaching them how to harness their knowledge as a resource for good. Together, we delivered care to those in greatest need and took meaningful steps toward closing the gaps in access and the global reach of healthcare. This awakening became one of their most powerful motivations—an inspiration that continues to fuel their commitment to those students who participated in serving communities and giving back.

Reflecting on your experiences is like reconnecting with old friends who once taught you invaluable lessons—some deeply personal, others undeniably painful, yet all shaping your journey. Revisiting these moments invites thoughtful introspection and offers the chance to glean wisdom from the chapters you've lived.

To achieve this, you must rely on your most valuable asset: the ability to think deeply. Focusing on positive thinking—by which I mean the kind that prompts you to examine both your strengths and weaknesses, uncover your true potential, and explore your options—cultivates a unique sense of self-awareness.

For a leader, self-awareness is essential. The more attuned you are to your own motivations and reasoning, the better equipped you become to guide yourself through each decision-making process. Most importantly, self-awareness opens the door to genuine connections with others, grounded in empathy, respect, and collaboration—which in my opinion is the very foundation of conscious leadership.

The Process of Thinking: From Pen to Paper

I find myself thinking constantly, just as you do. I try my best to enjoy and learn from this process. Sometimes, a nice long walk helps support my thinking process. Other times, I sit on my couch with a freshly brewed cup of coffee to think and reflect on any situation that I would like to find some solution to. Other times, I listen to music to provide me with the inspiration and comfort that I need to think. One essential tool in my process is my notepad – writing down my thoughts and reflections allows me to revisit ideas and discover strategies or solutions with greater clarity.

Thinkers are, in essence, writers as well. Many of the books ever published originate from the process of deep thinking, with creativity being its most significant outcome. That's exactly the right word—creativity. While I often viewed thinking primarily as a tool for developing strategies and solutions, I overlooked the fact that this process is inherently creative. When you consider it, writers are individuals who channel their thoughts into creativity, essentially thinking out loud through their words. Every time you engage in the process of deep thinking, you're crafting something new—whether it's a narrative, a solution, or a pathway to achieving your goals.

The thinking process does not necessarily have to be solitary; you can bring others with you. As someone who values inclusion, collaboration, and the importance of different points of view, I actively involve others in my process making thinking not just a personal journey but a collective effort. There are situations where I gathered the thoughts of friends. By the way, I do not invite all my friends to be part of this process, just the ones that can provide me with non-judgmental feedback. In this process, I do not call a meeting to order – like in our regular business meetings - but I call each of them separately to get their thoughts. For example, once I determine whom I will approach for a conversation, I begin by preparing a thoughtful set of questions. These questions are designed not only to assess their willingness and availability to offer feedback, but also to invite their perspectives on the situation. It is important that through this process I feel safe and valued. You'll be surprised by all that you can get, from insights, and perspectives from your friends. Not only you learned about you but also about them.

Throughout this process, my notepad is invaluable—I use it to capture my thoughts and the answers to guiding questions. Let me share how my thinking process unfolds. It begins with a conscious decision to reflect on the situation at hand. While I realize that circumstances can arise in an instant, it is crucial to stop as soon as you recognize something significant is happening. Next, I pick up my notepad and describe the situation in detail, capturing everything that's on my mind. By putting my thoughts into words, I'm able to clarify how I truly see the situation and better understand my own perspective. In these moments, I ask myself: What is this situation all about? What am I feeling right now? What emotions are surfacing? This initial self-inquiry builds the awareness I need to respond thoughtfully rather than react impulsively. I also consider: What lesson can I learn from this? What will my attitude toward this situation be like? Is this an issue I should work through alone, or would it be helpful to seek input from others? Is my thinking process aligned with my core values?

With these insights in hand, I begin to explore possible ways to address the situation and clarify what my role should be. This is a process I return to time and time again. Gaining clarity about my role allows me to view the issue from multiple angles, fostering both perspective and self-compassion—qualities that are especially important when navigating challenges. Once I've reflected on these aspects, I move on to evaluating my options and considering the potential outcomes of each choice.

By consistently using this approach, I've found that each time I face a difficult decision, the structure and clarity my notepad brings become even more valuable. In fact, let me share a personal example of how this practice guided me through one of the most pivotal moments in my life when I faced a major life decision. The questions were should I stay in my home country to continue my education, or should I step away from the comfort of my family and pursue new opportunities abroad? Being a first-generation student, the fear of the unknown was real and overwhelming. I remember feeling stuck, unsure of which path would be best for my future. In the midst of this uncertainty, I reached for my trusted notepad – the same one that I had used for countless reflections before. I began by writing out my thoughts and describing the situation in detail. The act of putting pen to paper helped me make sense of the swirling emotions and questions in my mind. I carefully listed the pros, cons and risks for each choice: remaining in my homeland or venturing out into the world. On one side, I wrote about the comfort of home, the support of family, and the familiarity of my surroundings.

On the other hand, I considered the excitement of new experiences, the challenge of adapting to a different culture, and the opportunities for personal growth. As I worked through this list, I realized the importance of gathering insights from others who had walked similar paths. I thought about friends who were studying both in Puerto Rico and overseas, and I reached out to a few for advice. Their perspectives gave me practical tips and emotional reassurance, helping me face my fears and see the possibilities more clearly. Through this process-reflecting in my notepad and seeking guidance – I gained the confidence to make an informed decision. In the end, the simple act of writing and connecting with others transformed my anxiety into clarity, and I was able to move forward with a sense of purpose and courage.

The Thinker Process as a Shield of Protection

Thinking serves not only to create awareness but also as a means of problem-solving and self-discovery. Thinking can serve as a protective shield in challenging situations, particularly on those that questioned your self-worth and contribution. By relying on deep thinking, you become better equipped to handle criticism or setbacks with grace and compassion. Instead of allowing negative experiences to undermine your confidence, you use introspection to extract valuable lessons and reinforce your sense of self. The process of thinking as a shield of protection can help you to maintain composure, build emotional resilience and guard you against making emotional or impulsive decisions that might not serve your best interest.

We come to recognize that our sense of self-worth is often shaped by how others perceive us. In the workplace, these influences might come from supervisors, directors, or colleagues, while at home, friends and family members can play a similar role. We must keep in mind that people's perceptions, judgements and even their limitations are constructs.

How many times have we found ourselves in situations where our worth is questioned? This can happen in subtle ways – perhaps through a dismissive glance, or when an idea you share during a meeting is met with indifference or outright skepticism. I remember vividly, especially in the early years of my career, how these moments would surface.

Despite my preparation and value I brought to the table, I often felt invisible. My contributions were overlooked or, at times, dismissed with a curt, "I don't understand you, could you repeat that?" It was as if my presence and insights were not fully recognized.

These interactions were not isolated. There seemed to be a pattern – a particular individual in the room would routinely skip over me when I raised my hand, or after I presented my thoughts, would respond in a way that made me doubt myself. Their feedback made me question whether my ideas were truly valuable or if there was something about my delivery – my accent perhaps -that made me less understandable or credible.

Driven by a growing sense of impostor syndrome, I began seeking validation from others in the same meeting. I would quietly ask colleagues afterwards, "Did my idea make sense? Was I clear?" Their reassurances helped me momentarily, but the self-doubt lingered. I started to wonder: Was it really about my ideas, or was I internalizing someone else's limitations? As you know, eventually, I turned to my notepad as a means of processing these feelings. I described each situation in detail, asking myself pointed questions: What exactly happened? What am I feeling right now? What emotions are coming up for me? This practice of self-inquiry became my lifeline – it created space for awareness and allowed me to respond with intention rather than react out of hurt. Through this reflection, I challenged myself to consider: what lessons can I learn from this experience? How do I want to show up next time? What attitude will best serve me and my values in these moments?

Over time, engaging in this process taught me to face my own fears and insecurities with compassion and respect. I realized that the actions or judgments of others do not define my value or merits of my ideas. By approaching myself with kindness and curiosity, I was able to reclaim my voice and strengthen my resilience. In doing so, I began to view these challenging moments not as indictments of my worth but as opportunities for growth and self-affirmation. This shift empowered me not only to navigate professional setbacks with greater confidence but also to extend understanding and empathy to others who may be facing similar doubts.

In academia, for instance, value is measured not only by the grants one secures for the institution, but also by the research and scholarship one produces and shares with the world. When submitting your work for promotion, you are at the mercy of a panel whose judgment, in a single decision, determines your professional value.

I remember one particular year, the sort of year in academia that feels like the culmination of every long night, research projects, and committed act of teaching. With hope and cautious optimism, I prepared my application for promotion, pouring my energy into every section. I believed, perhaps naively, that my dedication and sustained effort would be recognized—that the community I served would see the value I strived to bring with each day. I carried that hope into my supervisor's office, accomplishments arranged neatly in a binder, ready to share the story of my year's work. I spoke about my scholarship and the impact I tried to make; my words filled with pride and vulnerability. The response I received landed like a cold wind: *"Your scholarship does not reflect academic excellence."* In that instant, it was as though the ground beneath me had given way. Those words echoed, stripping away months of confidence in a matter of seconds. I could feel self-doubt creeping in, the familiar voice of impostor syndrome whispering that maybe I had fooled myself all along. Was I truly making a difference, or had I overestimated my own worth?

At that moment, I forced myself to reflect. Before reacting, I sat with the sting of those words, allowing myself a few heartbeats to simply notice what I was feeling. What was this pain telling me? I asked myself: What am I truly feeling right now? How do I perceive my contributions—not as measured by a single comment, but by the ongoing work and relationships I had built over time? I realized that practicing self-compassion was essential; I had to treat myself with empathy, acknowledging the difficulty of the feedback but refusing to let it define my entire identity or value.

I reminded myself that critical remarks—even the harsh ones—are sometimes more a reflection of the evaluator's lens than a true measure of my efforts. Instead of internalizing negativity or allowing it to spiral into self-criticism, I focused on the real impact of my work. The projects that helped students, the research that sparked dialogue, the dedication I brought every day—these were the truths I chose to hold onto. Through self-inquiry and gentle honesty with myself, I protected my sense of self-worth, allowing my awareness to serve as a shield, and reframed the moment as an opportunity to reaffirm my values and re-silience. Ultimately, I learned that my contribution was not diminished by one person's opinion, and that my intrinsic value was—and is—rooted in the quiet persistence and intention I bring to my work each day.

Epictetus once observed that, "When something happens, the only thing in your power is your attitude towards it—you can either accept it or resent it." Reflecting on his wisdom, it becomes clear that embracing acceptance in the face of what cannot be changed is the key to greater happiness and resilience. By choosing to approach life's challenges with acceptance, we draw strength from our intrinsic worth and find the capacity to cope positively, even amidst adversity.

The thinking process serves not only as a means of problem-solving and self-discovery but also acts as a protective shield in challenging circumstances. When faced with adversity or uncertainty, engaging in thoughtful reflection allows you to assess situations from multiple perspectives and respond consciously rather than react. Doing this helps you to stay calm, strengthen your emotional resilience, and protect yourself from making impulsive decisions that may not align with your best interests or your core values.

When the Thinker Navigates Organizational Change

In my experience as a mentor of others in higher education, I remember a dear colleague who once came to me seeking advice about his work experience. In his story, he still remembers the day that changed the course of his professional life. It began like any other morning at work, but before he could settle into his routine, he was unexpectedly summoned to a meeting. He recalled that the air in the room was tense, and as he sat down, he sensed that something significant was unfolding. The news was delivered swiftly and without warning: the organization was undergoing a major restructuring, and the position he had held for years was being reassigned. He listened, stunned, as it was explained that his responsibilities would be handed over to someone else. Meanwhile, he was being reassigned to a different position within the organization.

He remembered how a wave of emotions washed over him—confusion, disappointment, and disbelief—as the details of the change became clear. His role hadn't been eliminated, but it was evident that his contributions over the years were being quietly set aside. There was no explanation for the decision, no acknowledgment of the countless hours, sacrifices, or passion he had poured into his work.

In that moment, the pride he once felt in his work gave way to a sense of loss. The lack of empathy and communication from leadership made it seem as if all his dedication had been for nothing. He couldn't help but wonder how many others had felt this same sting of being undervalued—how many passionate professionals had left their organizations under similar circumstances, driven away by decisions that ignored their hard work and commitment.

In my role as a mentor, reflecting on his experience, I realized that true leadership is not just a skill or an innate talent. Rather, it is anchored in intangible qualities—the ability to stay connected to your core values, to draw on the lessons instilled through your upbringing, and to approach every situation with empathy, respect, and genuine curiosity. These attributes are what make us human, and as I continue my journey, they are the qualities I strive to embody and to recognize in those around me.

These very traits are what render a leader both human and thoughtful. Faced with such upheaval, how does one respond? It's natural to wade through sadness and disappointment—emotions that all of us encounter. Yet, it's crucial to recognize these feelings and set boundaries, ensuring they don't define our path forward. Consider asking yourself: What options do I truly have? Should I stay and seek ways to thrive, depart and embrace new opportunities, or choose a creative approach? While our instincts may pull us toward the first two choices, imagine the liberation that comes with exploring innovative alternatives. The more creative your choices, the greater the sense of freedom you can cultivate.

Let's break down my approach to handling any type of situation. First and foremost, what am I feeling right now? What emotions are surfacing? What will my attitude toward this situation be like? Is this an issue I should work through alone, or would it be helpful to seek input from others? It's essential to treat yourself with compassion and recognize that you are capable of finding solutions to your challenges. Practicing self-compassion means acknowledging your current feelings, allowing yourself to sit with discomfort, and remaining open to change. In my experience, every situation brings about some form of change.

Early in my professional journey, I found that whenever challenges arose, my initial instinct was to resist and let my emotions dictate my response. Looking back, I can see that this approach rarely led to positive outcomes. Life is unpredictable, and sometimes you're faced with situations you never imagined.

One Friday morning, the sky over New York was heavy with rain—one of those relentless storms that seem to settle over the city and refuse to let up. The weather reports warned of severe rainfall across the tri-state area, but many of us assumed it would pass quickly, just another rainy day. We couldn't have anticipated what was coming. When we returned to work on Monday, we were met with the shocking reality that our entire building had suffered extensive water damage. The infrastructure was compromised, and we had to vacate immediately, with discussions underway about relocating the entire clinic.

As the administrator, I felt overwhelmed by the enormity of the situation. Questions swirled through my mind: Where would we go? What would happen to our patients and staff? The uncertainty triggered a flood of emotions—confusion, worry, and frustration. Yet, amid the chaos, I asked myself the most important question: What is this situation truly about? This moment of self-inquiry happened in a matter of minutes, but it changed my approach.

Recognizing the gravity of the crisis, I gave myself permission to step back and reflect before reacting. I realized that there was no need for an immediate response; taking a moment of silence allowed me to process the situation fully. Over the course of the day, clarity emerged. I devised a plan for the next steps, secured the support of the staff and administration, and found a way forward. This experience reinforced the importance of awareness and thoughtful reflection in navigating unexpected challenges.

To illustrate how these lessons on reflection and self-compassion play out in real life, let me share a friend's pivotal experience that resonates with the earlier narrative. Not long ago, I spoke with a close friend who experienced a remarkably similar event—once again, the root cause, in my opinion, was a profound lack of communication and empathy from the organizational leadership. To protect my friend's privacy, I'll refer to him as VJ.

For the past two decades, VJ worked at an organization, often describing his role as deeply fulfilling and instrumental in his professional growth. Over the decades, VJ contributed to and led significant projects that safeguarded the organization's history, earning widespread recognition as an expert in the field. The shock came when VJ discovered, with little warning, that the organization had offered 'packages' to many in his department, essentially incentivizing them to leave because the department was about to be dismantled. Suddenly, VJ's position was no longer deemed essential, and they were strongly encouraged to either accept the severance package or leave with nothing.

Facing the prospect of unemployment after years of loyalty—and at a stage of life when such changes can be particularly daunting, VJ grappled with difficult questions: What options do I truly have? Should I depart and seek new opportunities, or is there space for a creative path forward? Would my age be an obstacle? Am I still employable? These are questions that we all asked ourselves. Facing a sudden change in his job and possible impact on his finances was not in his plans, he must take a decision.

A few weeks ago, during our usual morning coffee, I sat down with VJ once more. He shared that after weeks of reflection, he chose not to view his situation as a forced retirement, but instead as an opportunity to pursue a more creative path. Drawing on his extensive academic background, professional experience, and well-earned reputation, VJ decided to embark on a new adventure—one fueled by his own expertise, passion, and determination. What initially felt like the end of a career soon transformed into the beginning of a new chapter, both professionally and personally. Bravo, VJ!

Often, our attachment to a particular role or situation is anchored in fear of change and uncertainty about what the future may hold. Sometimes, it is also rooted in the comfort—or even complacency—that comes from many years spent in the same environment: a little over a decade in the first scenario, over two decades for VJ in the second. In both cases, they were prompted to ask themselves meaningful questions, sparking a thoughtful evaluation of possible next steps. This process led them to explore a range of options. The more alternatives we allow ourselves, the more agency we gain over our destinies. While we cannot control every aspect of the future, we do possess the power to choose our path and shape the unfolding chapters of our lives.

When the Thinker Seeks for Meaning and Purpose

Discovering meaning in our actions is fundamental—it's what fuels our purpose and clarifies the mission we are called to pursue. My decision to enter healthcare was rooted in a deep sense of vocation, something that transcends mere commitment and feels almost sacred. This understanding was imparted to me by my mother. I still recall my childhood medical visits, when our trusted physician conveyed an unmistakable sense of genuine care. After each appointment, my mother would remark, "This doctor truly has the vocation—God bless him." That memory has stayed with me, shaping my belief that vocation is not just a duty but a calling to serve with authenticity and heart.

It's often true that we spend more time at work than in our own homes, sometimes even more than with our families. Many of us dedicate years to pursuing and developing what we believe to be our passion or vocation—yet, in the process, it's all too easy to lose ourselves in the name of our profession. Sometimes, we even forget how to find joy in what we do.

At times, our sense of meaning and purpose can be overshadowed by ego. Consider the realm of leadership: while leading others can be deeply rewarding, it also carries the risk of becoming restrictive—particularly when authority inflates ego and a desire for power. We've all seen situations where individuals, upon stepping into leadership, allow their attitudes and communication to shift. They may become protective of their knowledge, reluctant to share, fearing that openness might threaten their position. This mindset, rooted in self-preservation, often builds walls instead of bridges. Reflecting on these dynamics, I ask: Are you truly prepared to set aside your ego and move beyond self-preservation? Can you mentor others sincerely, without expecting anything in return? What are you willing to compromise?

Regardless of profession or ambition, we often become so focused on achieving success that we lose sight of the joy inherent in our work. I encourage everyone to embrace opportunities to use their expertise as a resource for good. I've always said happiness comes when you turn your knowledge into a resource. If you are a healthcare provider, consider joining outreach programs and making a tangible difference, as I have experienced firsthand. For educators, teaching should go beyond imparting knowledge—it should be a journey of empowering others to educate themselves. If you are a leader, mentor someone, pass on your wisdom, and ensure that your philosophy and legacy endure through others. By sharing knowledge and nurturing growth, you not only enrich the lives of those around you but also find deeper fulfillment in your own journey.

When the Thinker Faces Vulnerability

One of the greatest challenges we face is not always the situation itself, but the vulnerability it brings and how we choose to accept it. Failures and feelings of inadequacy often test our resolve. For example, think about the times you've forgotten to respond to an important email, resulting in a project delay. Let's break down this scenario: imagine you missed replying to a confirmation email about shipping a crucial product, and now you have to explain the situation to your supervisor and the team. First, ask yourself, "What am I feeling right now?" Next, consider, "What should I do next?" Should you accept responsibility, or search for an excuse to justify your oversight? What's the right way to handle this?

It's a tough situation, isn't it? Instead of circling around possible explanations—or even fabricating reasons—you choose honesty. You address your supervisor and team directly, saying: "I want to acknowledge and apologize for not following up on the confirmation email, which led to the delay of the product we've all been working on for months. I appreciate everyone's commitment to this project as we work together to find a solution."

By responding this way, your vulnerability demonstrates accountability, humility, and openness. This approach fosters trust and strengthens your relationship with both your supervisor and your team.

The Thinker: How Reflection Evolves Into Leadership

In the journey from self-reflection to leadership, I have found that genuine growth is rooted in the willingness to examine both personal and professional experiences. This process is more than a skill—it's a mindset, one that demands self-awareness, empathy, and a steady respect for oneself and for those around us. True leadership, I realized, is not measured by accomplishments alone but by an ongoing commitment to one's values and to serving others with humanity.

At the heart of this path lies self-awareness. Knowing my own strengths and confronting my limitations has given me the perspective to make considered decisions and to form relationships grounded in authenticity. I have learned that while intelligence and integrity are essential traits, the context in which we lead—the environment, the team, the culture—can shape our approach as much as any inherent quality.

Often, change—whether in life or in the workplace—stirs up uncertainty and emotion. Yet, I have seen firsthand that such moments can spark new ideas and opportunities. Leadership, for me, is about balancing compassion for others with the ability to value myself and maintain healthy boundaries. This equilibrium is what allows a leader to respond to challenges with both empathy and clarity.

Inevitably, criticism and feedback come our way, sometimes shaking our confidence. In those moments, nurturing self-worth and practicing self-compassion have helped me stay centered. It is through adversity that I have built resilience—adapting, learning, and emerging with a deeper sense of purpose.

There is something transformative about discovering purpose in the work you do. It infuses daily tasks with meaning and guides your decisions. Developing empathy and emotional intelligence has been crucial for me in building supportive teams and forging relationships that matter.

Throughout my career, I have recognized that being a "Thinker" is not a set formula to follow, but a daily practice—one that emerges naturally in the ebb and flow of life. When faced with an unexpected challenge—a missed deadline, a tough conversation, or a setback—I learned the importance of reflection not as a separate activity, but as something intertwined with action. In these moments, writing became my anchor. By putting my thoughts on paper, I could untangle worries, identify what truly mattered, and move forward with clarity. This simple act of writing helped transform crises into actionable steps.

Over time, I have come to understand that the "Thinker" doesn't search for the perfect answer or follow a rigid set of rules. It's about being honest with yourself, reflecting on experience, and then inviting others into that process—sharing lessons learned, seeking dialogue, and growing together.

For me, the act of thinking bridges the gap between introspection and meaningful action. Through writing and open conversations, leadership becomes an ongoing practice—guided by integrity, humility, and a genuine concern for others, rather than a pursuit of authority.

In the end, I have learned that thinking—anchored in honest self-reflection and enriched by the perspectives of others—enables leaders to act with compassion and conviction. Through this practice, we find the strength to adapt, the vision to overcome challenges, and the inspiration to support those around us. That, I believe, is the true humanistic foundation of leadership.

CHAPTER SEVEN

The Thinking Life

Denise Nelson Nash

Thinking in time requires holding past, present, and future at once. Thinking with uncertainty requires letting go of all three.

The Thinking Life

"You summarize the text well, but your analysis could go further — what deeper meaning or implication do you see here?"

My high school English teacher wrote this across my heavily red-lined paper with so many comments that my original writing was barely visible. I remember shrinking in my seat as my eyes skimmed over the marked-up pages. I thought I had written a good paper, not great, but good. I read the book, responded to the assignment questions, and wrote a paper. Wasn't that thinking?

But my teacher's comments told me something very different. Each comment led me to something I hadn't discovered yet: there are different types of thinking. I was summarizing what I read when the assignment called for analytical thinking, interpretive thinking, and critical thinking. I was using one tool, when many tools were needed. My teacher was prompting me to dig deeper – to become a Thinker.

The red-lined paper haunted me for many more assignments after that. After several more assignments, it came into focus what my teacher was trying to teach me: thinking isn't one thing. It's many things. And knowing which type of thinking a moment requires takes practice.

Knowing which type of thinking to use is a part of leadership. Leaders often solve when they should be exploring. With all the types of thinking available to us — analytical, critical, generative, systems, linear versus non-linear, reflexive — why does it sometimes seem so difficult to collect our thoughts, navigate the mental obstacles, and create a relationship with thinking?

I suggest that thinking requires cross-training. Just like athletes develop different muscle groups for different sports, thinkers need to call on different types of thinking and different combinations depending on the situation. While tennis players lift weights to build strength and swim to improve their cardiovascular fitness and upper body strength, basketball players focus on building strength and explosive power through plyometrics and exercise drills. Both sports require mental agility and focus. Quick decisions may need reflexive thinking. New ideas and novel problems may need divergent or creative thinking. Complex situations may need a combination or synthesis of many thinking types. The athlete knows this, so does the Thinker.

Learning to recognize which type of thinking is needed takes practice. You won't always choose correctly—I'm still practicing.

This chapter explores what I've learned about that practice, sometimes stumbling into situations where my usual way of thinking failed me. As you read, notice: Which comes naturally to you? Which feels uncomfortable? This is about choosing your own adventure with thinking.

Thinking Story: Echoes and Ripples

Thinking Across Time

I was twenty-nine when I became the director of a community school of the performing and visual arts. On my first day, I could sense it — something underneath the warm welcome. The team I inherited had worked together for years.

Two full-time administrators and more than fifteen part-time teachers, all of whom had worked together for years. They had unspoken ways of doing things, rhythms, and shared history. And I was the newbie.

Pause moment: Think about a time you were the newbie and joined a team or organization. Could you sense something about its history? Were there unspoken ways of doing things? How did this shape how people responded to you?

Back to my story

In the first staff meeting, I outlined the charge I was given to identify new revenue streams, expand enrollment, and expand program offerings. I felt the need to prove myself and the pressure to produce results; to show I had creativity, vision, and the ability to elevate the program. I presented a few ideas that I thought were reasonable. The response was polite. Too polite. Heads nodded. No one disagreed. But there was clearly a discomfort in the politeness. My attempts at facilitating an exploratory conversation of ideas drifted along with no shared idea generation.

I remember leaving the meeting confused. I'd done what I thought leaders do, brought vision and proposed solutions forward that could be discussed collaboratively. So, why the disconnection?

A week or so later, one of the teachers stopped by my office and asked to speak with me. She was one of the teachers who had been with the program for more than a decade. She asked if she could be honest with me. I braced myself for what was coming next.

She told me that the last director had a lot of ideas too. Some good ones, but they came fully formed without an opportunity for input. There were a number of times, the staff would walk into meetings and find out decisions had already been made. After a while they stopped offering suggestions, since their ideas didn't seem to matter.

That's when I felt the weight of the past

It wasn't just history in an abstract way, but experiences of decisions that had left people feeling unheard. The teacher wasn't complaining.

She was caring. Caring for the program. Caring and hoping I would be different. The past wasn't just background; it was shaping the present and creating patterns I was already repeating without realizing it.

I had arrived in the role thinking I needed to solve the program's challenges: revenue, enrollment, and reach. But the real challenge was temporal. I was focused on the future without understanding the past or truly seeing the present.

My high school English teacher would have recognized my mistake. I was summarizing the situation, when I needed to be analyzing it. So, I started asking different questions. Not strategic questions but historical questions about the team and their experiences: "What's worked well in the past?" "What hasn't?" "What decisions are the team still living with?" "What would you change if you could?"

The conversations that followed revealed hidden layers. Previous directors who made unilateral decisions. Programs that launched with fanfare, then quietly discontinued when the resources dried up. Families leaving disappointed in the program and staff cynical about future promises — I had stepped in it without taking the time to see the warnings. The team showed me the echoes I needed to hear.

I realized my job wasn't to present solutions but to understand what was already present, both the visible and the invisible consequences of the past, before future imagining. So instead of offering ideas, I asked the team to plan with me. To figure things out together. We worked together in small groups and as a whole. The energy changed. Politeness gave way to enthusiasm, which carried over into the classroom and into the community. We were generating ideas while rebuilding trust.

Thinking across time involves projecting forward, while understanding the past and present. It's asking questions: *If we do this now, what happens in six months? One year? Two years? Would it be better to launch small and grow gradually, or launch big and take a risk of failure? Are we solving today's problem in a way that creates a problem for the future? If we start it, can we sustain it?*

We made decisions together. Small sustainable initiatives grew into signature programs. Families told other families. Engagement and enrollment grew. A new reliable revenue stream was created. The culture shifted from protecting what was to imagining what could be. The trust built created ripples.

I left the position after four years. We had achieved what I was tasked with on my first day. It was an example of Mary Parker Follett's concept of "power with." Shared decision-making and the collective control of the situation led to empowerment. What I remember years later is not the growth in the program, not the new revenue streams, but the trust, shared ownership, and collective creativity that came from thinking in time together.

Thinking in time remains part of my practice to this day. I've learned to pause and ask: *What past might be shaping the present? What is needed in this moment? What will this decision set in motion?*

This is Thinking in Time, holding multiple temporalities at once and paving the way for the wisdom to emerge.

When the Map Has No Roads

Thinking with Uncertainty

Thinking in time requires holding past, present, and future at once. Thinking with uncertainty requires letting go of all three. COVID-19 taught me this.

In March 2020, I was a senior administrator at a small residential college when COVID-19 arrived. We were having the normal conversations about the semester and planning for the next. In a matter of weeks everything stopped. We closed residence halls, shuttered offices, sent students and employees home, and moved courses online. No one had a playbook for a global pandemic or what to do. The map literally had no roads.

Everyone in higher education has their own version of this story. This is mine.

I remember the first senior administrator emergency meetings. We were on Zoom. Lucky for us that we had been testing out the use of Zoom with our Trustee meetings, so there was some familiarity among us. This was not so for the faculty. Most of the faculty barely knew what Zoom was, let alone how to use it.

Then came the questions: *How long will this last? Can we bring students back in the fall? Will students come back in the fall? What about international students who can't get home? How do you teach a studio art class online? What about students without reliable internet at home? What about…. What about…. What about….?*

Nobody had answers. The not knowing for a group of seasoned senior administrators, including me, was disorienting. We had no precedent to draw on, no way to think through something that had never happened before. My first instinct was to analyze the situation and gather data. Create plans and contingency plans. But there was a problem. How do you analyze a pandemic nobody understands? How do you plan when information is changing hourly?

I tried anyway. Our work was divided into domains with each senior administrator assigned a domain. I, along with my colleagues, created spreadsheets tracking COVID related impacts, such as academic spaces, residential hall safe living, diving safe meal groups, asset acquisitions, testing, isolation spaces, communications — there was a domain, sub-group, and spreadsheet for everything we could possibly think of. I drafted plans and contingency plans for scenarios. I met with team members to coordinate response plans. But every plan was obsolete within days. I was trying to think through uncertainty using tools designed for certainty, and it wasn't working.

Three or four weeks in, I was mid-sentence in another emergency meeting explaining scenario analysis number forty-seven when one of my colleagues interrupted me. "Can we stop pretending we know what we're doing?" Six administrator squares on Zoom, frozen mid-expression. Five seconds of silence felt like five minutes.

The Zoom screen lit up with thumbs up emojis and exhales. It was the moment we all needed. As seasoned administrators, our instinct was to fix, to problem-solve. The moment took me back to what my English teacher's red-lined paper told me years before, maybe not consciously, but there it was — sometimes you need to stop using the thinking tool you have and admit you need a different one. The thinking we needed had to be discovered.

So, I shifted from reactive planning to diverse thinking skills — enter cross-training. I practiced different kinds of thinking. With the paths unknown, I turned to exploratory thinking to move us through unmapped territory by trying things, noticing what happens, adjusting, and trying again.

One discovery that still stays with me: remote work. Before March 2020, I'd been one of those leaders who believed that face-to-face builds culture, and we need everyone on campus. After all, we were a residential college; being together was our brand.

A few months into the pandemic, one of our quietest staff members remarked that she had contributed more ideas in the last month than in the last three years. She was someone who always seemed somewhat disengaged in meetings. Turns out she was processing. Online, she would think before typing. She could participate within her introversion. These reports revealed a different possibility: *What if remote work isn't inferior, just different? What if it creates opportunities we hadn't imagined? What if I was wrong?*

I started noticing more. Employees with processing differences appreciated the remote options. Employees with family obligations could collaborate on projects while fulfilling coordination and scheduling needs. Remote wasn't worse, it was different. Different possibilities were created that we'd never explored before because we never had to.

Three months in we weren't pretending to have answers. I continued to plan while becoming more comfortable with iterative discovery. I tried something, learned from it, adjusted, and tried again. The discomfort of not knowing never fully went away, but it became tolerable. I was thinking with uncertainty. While I was just trying to keep my head above water, I didn't drown and that taught us something. I didn't have to have it all figured out.

A year later when vaccines arrived and we began to bring students and employees back to campus; we reflected on what we had learned. We asked: *What if we kept some of what we learned? What if we don't go back to exactly how things were before?* The conversation about what we might continue doing from this terrible time was one of the most interesting ones. We'd discovered things we wouldn't have been forced into unmapped territory. The question became: *Could we choose uncertainty on purpose? Could we explore without a crisis forcing us to?*

I don't know if we succeed in answering these questions – yet. Patterns are powerful. But I know something shifted in me. I became less afraid of uncertainty. I learned that it's ok to lean into unmapped territory and not panic if there isn't a road or a compass. I learned to ask myself what kind of thinking is needed in a given moment.

Sometimes analysis is needed. Sometimes strategy. Sometimes synthesis. But sometimes, it's the willingness to move forward not knowing what is needed. To try things. To learn from what happens. To adjust. To trust. To clarify. So, I continue to cross-train in my thinking practice.

At this point, you might be wondering what my cross-training thinking practice looks like. My daughter is a three-time All-American tennis player, so I will use the familiar sport that I spent so much time in the stands watching to provide a glimpse into my approach.

- Cross-training thinking starts with a diagnostic. Like the tennis player who has a dominant arm, we all have a go-to way of thinking:
- Analytical thinkers break things down into parts, seek data, want proof
- Intuitive thinkers trust their guts, recognize patterns quickly
- Convergent thinkers want to narrow things down, get to the right answers quickly
- Generative thinkers explore possibilities, focus on observations, resist structure
- Systems thinkers see the whole picture, look at the interconnected relationships
- Linear thinkers use logical, sequential, methodical approaches

There are many more types, but you get the picture.

Your dominant mode is the one that feels like "just thinking." The others feel like effort. I started by noticing which I reach for in meetings, in problem-solving, and in conversation. That was my tennis forehand. Once I recognized it, I knew what to cross-train against. Acknowledging that my dominant mode is generative thinking, I set an intention to use the full complement of thinking types—identifying what was needed when and why. I started by slowing down, way down, basically, I learned to stop myself from launching into the familiar and notice.

The Analogy

When faced with a problem or issue, I ask "what is this like?" and "have I seen something similar before?" A stalled project might be like a car stuck in mud, requiring traction (a different approach) rather than gunning it. A hiring decision is like casting a play, where skills matter but so does ensemble fit. I force myself to generate analogies before moving forward. This forces me to seek solutions outside my thinking comfort zone.

The Thinking Journal

At the end of the day, instead of replaying what went well or what didn't, I ask:
What did I assume without examining?
When or where did I feel defensive?
When did I avoid thinking about options?
This helps me become more aware of my blind spots. It's not easy or comfortable, but training never is.

The Pre-Mortem

We are all familiar with the post-mortem where we examine the successes, failures, and lessons learned. I like doing this in advance as a cross-training exercise. I practiced this in the re-telling of my first supervisory role where we explored questions like, "If we do this now, what happens in six months? One year? Two years?"

This is peering into the future asking what if questions - exploring, analyzing, interpreting, and using non-linear thinking. Leaping forward and backwards to see the big picture, links, and what ifs- "What could possibly go wrong?" It surfaces the risks your optimism obscures.

Thinking Partners

This is one of my favorite cross-training exercises. At least once a week, I puzzle out a problem with a colleague whose thinking style is different from mine. I listen without defending or resisting. As a generative thinker, I seek analytical, systematic, and linear-thinking partners. I am continually fascinated by our different natural modes, and I have strengthened my ability to use a particular mode or combination as my go-to in certain situations.

Content Consumption

I read. I read a lot, and I read content outside my sector weekly. My current role is in higher education governance. My primary daily consumption is focused on policy, practices, politics, and persistence. So, I read philosophy, fiction, and biographies. I listen to podcasts (I co-host a higher ed podcast and learn from our guests) on criminal investigations, influencers, and home renovations. Spending time with visual thinkers, deductive reasoners, and creative and conceptual analyzers enriches my training. I import different approaches and mental models from each. This is cross-training thinking.

The pandemic was a lesson in the usual ways of thinking that won't work here. So, what else will you try?

I'm still learning. I still reach for the familiar when I should be pushing myself to try the unfamiliar. But I've learned to notice when the map has no roads and to keep moving.

PART THREE

THE TINKERER

CHAPTER EIGHT

Igniting the Spark

Trisha Beck

The Tinkerer doesn't walk the trampled path.
The Tinkerer creates entirely new landscapes.

"Insanity is doing the same thing over and over again and expecting different results."

— Often attributed to Einstein (though he never said it)

The Monday morning meeting starts the same way it always does. I walk into the same conference room, the agenda is the same, and the same people are in attendance. The focus of the meeting is all of the change that is needed to improve the patient satisfaction scores. Ideas are shared but not embraced. Each point being made is met with a level of pontification from the audience. The same ideas each week, the same comments, the same conversations. There are no plans for action, just a plan to meet again.æ

There is an odd comfort in repetition. The well-worn path feels safe because you have walked it before. The familiarity of your routine requires little to no thought, no risk, no uncomfortable uncertainty. Autopilot mode promises predictability: why reinvent the wheel when you can just execute what's proven?

But here's the secret about the well-worn path: it is not taking you anywhere. Yes, you are in motion. You are busy. You are working hard. But the well-worn path is a treadmill, all movement, no progress. And still you wonder why the results don't change. You have become the leader who does the same thing over and over expecting different results.

Becoming a Tinkerer breaks that cycle. Progress doesn't come from doing the same thing better. It comes from doing different things, learning what works, and pivoting.

In a world that changes daily, flexibility isn't enough. You need to be fluid, completely reshaping your approach rather than bending slightly. You need to confront the fear that keeps you stagnant and find the courage to become something new. You must slow down to gain speed.

The Tinkerer doesn't walk the trampled path. The Tinkerer creates new landscapes.

The Pin

Remember my mentor, the pediatrician CEO who transformed me into a Learner? He wore a pin on his white coat. Red circle. A red line slashed through it. And inside, the words: "We have Always Done It This Way."

I noticed it during one of his visits to my office, right before he launched into his usual barrage of questions. "Why do we discharge patients at noon?" "Why don't we allow family members in the ICU overnight?" "Can we do this process differently?"

After he left, I found myself staring at where he had been standing, thinking about that pin. A banned phrase. The most dangerous words in healthcare, literally crossed out on his chest. But here is what I didn't understand yet: he wasn't just wearing it as a message to others. He was wearing it as a reminder to himself.

Years later, after I had grown from that intimidated new leader into someone confident enough to ask my own questions, I commented on the pin. "How long have you worn that?" "Twenty-three years," he said. "I started wearing it the day after I caught myself saying those exact words in a meeting."

He had been sharing the patient rounding structure, and a senior physician had suggested modifications. His immediate, reflexive response had been: "We have always done it this way." The words were out of his mouth before he realized. And in that moment, he realized he had become the very obstacle he had spent his career trying to remove.

So he had the pin made and wore it every day. A physical reminder that the moment you stop tinkering, the moment you start defending the status quo simply because it is the status quo, you have stopped leading.

"I wear it," he told me, "because I never want to forget that 'we have always done it this way' is not a reason. It is an excuse." He didn't just ask questions to make me learn. He asked questions to keep himself tinkering. Every "Why do we…?" was him testing whether our current approach still made sense, or whether we were just walking the well-worn path out of habit.

The pin crossed out complacency. A line through the phrase that kills innovation, that stops progress, that turns leaders into guards of the past instead of architects of the future. I think about that pin often now, especially when I feel myself reaching for the comfort of the familiar. When I am tempted to defend a process simply because it exists, or dismiss a new idea because the old one is working "well enough."

The Tinkerer doesn't just tolerate questions. The Tinkerer invites them, pursues them, celebrates them. Because questions are how you avoid becoming your own obstacle. My mentor taught me to be a Learner through his questions. But he taught me to be a Tinkerer through his pin and through his relentless willingness to question even his own assumptions.

I don't wear a pin. But I carry his lesson: the most dangerous distance in leadership is the distance between "this works" and "this is the only way." The Tinkerer closes that gap by never stopping asking: "Can we do this better or differently?" Even when the answer might require tinkering with something that is working just fine.

Fear as Fuel

Why do intelligent, capable leaders keep walking the same path when it is clearly not working? Fear.

Not the fear that makes your heart race in danger. The subtle fear of change itself. Of the unknown. Of trying something new. This fear keeps you exactly as you are. Forever. It convinces you that consistency is virtue and change is dangerous. That the well-worn path is well-worn for a reason. Fear promises safety but delivers stagnation.

The Tinkerer feels this fear too. But they have learned to recognize it not as a warning to stop, but as a signal they're on the edge of growth. So they lean in.

The Tinkerer has the courage to admit they don't know. The bravery to try something knowing it might fail. The humility to say to their team, "Let's try this and see what happens," without the armor of certainty.

This vulnerability terrifies most leaders. We are supposed to have the answers. Admitting we are experimenting feels like weakness. But vulnerability isn't weakness. Instead it is the doorway to growth. When you are willing to tinker, to test, to try things that might not work, you unlock discovery.

Here is the secret: It's exhilarating! There is an energy that comes from experimentation. A thrill in trying something new. An excitement in discovering what works and what doesn't.

Watch a Tinkerer's eyes light up talking about an experiment that flopped but taught them something. Listen to the energy in their voice describing a new approach. Feel the momentum they create inviting their team into the adventure of figuring things out together.

This isn't the exhausted energy of running faster on a treadmill. This is the alive, buzzing, creative energy of exploration. Of discovery. Of building something new.

The Tinkerer has learned there is more joy in one meaningful experiment than in a thousand repetitions of the same routine. More satisfaction in learning what doesn't work than pretending what used to work still does. More excitement in "let's see what happens" than in the false security of "we have always done it this way."

They trade the comfort of certainty for the thrill of discovery. They have discovered that the energy of experimentation is more sustaining than the exhaustion of repetition. That the vulnerability of not knowing is more honest than false certainty. That the bravery to try something new is more rewarding than staying safe.

The Tinkerer doesn't just break the cycle through courage. They break it by falling in love with tinkering itself. The question isn't whether you will feel the fear. The question is whether you will lean into it, embrace the vulnerability it requires, and discover the exhilaration waiting on the other side.

The Hummingbird's Dance

Now picture a hummingbird. Watch it approach a flower. It doesn't land and settle in. It hovers, wings beating 80 times per second, making constant adjustments to stay perfectly positioned. Every flower is different. Different angles. Different depth. Different shapes. The hummingbird must adapt in real-time, adjusting its approach with precision.

Here is what you probably noticed, the hummingbird never stops moving. Wings blur. Hovering at a flower for just seconds before darting to the next and then the next. Visiting hundreds of flowers in a single morning, each one requiring a completely different approach. Watch closer. What looks like chaos is actually something else entirely. That hummingbird? It's tinkering.

Every flower presents a new problem to solve. This one is a trumpet flower, long, narrow, deep as a test tube. The hummingbird must insert its beak perfectly straight, no room for error, reaching three inches down to find nectar. One degree off and it hits the wall. Too shallow and it gets nothing.

That one is a drooping fuchsia, petals hanging down like a bell. The hummingbird must flip completely upside down, hovering inverted, defying what seems possible. What worked at the trumpet flower is useless here.

This one is a salvia, side-facing, petals wide. Approach from below and you miss it entirely. From above and the petals block access. The hummingbird must come in laterally, wings compensating for the awkward angle.

The hummingbird doesn't have a master plan. It doesn't walk into the garden with a predetermined strategy. It doesn't convene a committee to decide the optimal approach before taking action. It just tries things. Approach this flower from below. Didn't work? Try from the side. Still not right? Flip upside down. There it is.

The hummingbird gathers feedback instantly. Every millisecond provides data. Wing angle wrong? Adjust. Distance off? Recalibrate.

Position awkward? Reshape completely. This is tinkering in its purest form. Small experiments. Rapid iteration. Constant learning. No attachment to what worked at the last flower because this flower is different.

The hummingbird doesn't see failure. Instead it sees information. No shame. No fear of looking foolish. No paralysis from not having the perfect answer before starting. Just relentless, curious experimentation.

And here is what matters: what appears to be chaos produces precision. Not good enough positioning. Not close positioning. Perfect. The hummingbird's beak reaches exactly where it needs to reach. Its wings hold it exactly where it needs to be. Its body angles exactly as required.

How does chaos produce precision? Through constant adjustments. The hummingbird isn't precise because it planned everything perfectly upfront. It's precise because it adjusts hundreds of times per second. It tinkers its way to perfect positioning through relentless, real-time adaptation.

Now think about your leadership. How many times do you refuse to approach the problem until you have figured out the perfect strategy? How often do you convene another meeting, gather more data, wait for certainty before trying anything? How frequently do you take what worked in one situation and force it onto a completely different problem?

The hummingbird teaches us: precision comes from experimentation, not planning. Mastery comes from adjustment, not prediction. Success comes from trying, learning, and trying differently. The Tinkerer doesn't stand at the edge of the garden analyzing every flower before moving. The Tinkerer hovers, tries, adjusts, and moves to the next challenge. Wings blurring. Always in motion. Always learning.

My Hummingbird Morning

I learned to be a hummingbird during three back-to-back meetings. Three teams. Three hours. All facing the same performance issue on paper. I walked in with my standard leadership approach ready: review the data, identify gaps, develop action plans. One approach. One well-worn path.

The First team

I started my data review. Nobody was looking at the screen. They were looking at each other, tense, uncomfortable. The old me would have pushed through my agenda anyway. The Tinkerer adjusted. "What's actually going on here?"

Not a knowledge problem. A relationship problem. They didn't need my action plan. They needed to clear the air. I abandoned my prepared approach entirely. Facilitated, then got out of the way.

The Second team

Same metrics. I walked in ready to replicate what just worked—facilitate relationships. But this team wasn't tense. They were genuinely confused. "We thought we were doing everything right."

What worked twenty minutes ago? Useless here. The Tinkerer doesn't cling to the last success. I flipped completely. Taught instead of facilitated. Different flower, different approach.

The Third team

Same metrics. I walked in ready to either facilitate or teach—surely one of those would work. But this team wasn't fighting or confused. They were exhausted. "We know what to do. We just don't have the resources."

Neither approach fit. The Tinkerer experiments until something works. I stopped the meeting. "You don't need facilitation or teaching. You need me to fight for staffing." A third flower requiring a third completely different solution.

The leader walking the well-worn path would have used the same approach in all three rooms. Pushed through with the data review regardless of what was actually needed. Wondering why two out of three teams didn't improve.

The Tinkerer hovers close, senses what this specific situation requires, tries an approach, gathers immediate feedback, and adjusts without attachment to what worked before. That morning taught me: the skill isn't finding one perfect leadership approach. The skill is rapid experimentation and constant adaptation. Wings beating. Constantly sensing. Trying, adjusting, reshaping. No paralysis from not knowing the right answer before starting. No shame when the first approach doesn't work. No clinging to what succeeded in the last meeting because this meeting is different.

That's tinkering. Real-time. Relentless. Responsive. The hummingbird doesn't march through the garden with one predetermined strategy. It dances adjusting hundreds of times per second until it finds exactly what this flower needs. That's not chaos. That's mastery through tinkering.

Cooking Without a Recipe

Here is how Tinkerers actually make progress: they cook without a recipe, tasting and adjusting as they go. The first attempt is meant to teach you what the dish needs. You taste it, adjust the seasoning, and try again. Then again.

But unlike cooks who follow the recipe exactly, Tinkerers trust their palate. They ask not just "Does this need more salt?" but "What if this needs pepper instead of salt? What if we are making the wrong dish entirely?" Each taste teaches. Some adjustments work and become part of your cooking instinct. Others fail, teaching you what flavors don't combine. Some bites reveal you are cooking the wrong meal for this occasion and you need to start over with different ingredients. But every single adjustment adds to your culinary knowledge, your sense of what works.

When something doesn't taste right, whether it's slightly off or completely inedible the Tinkerer asks: "What's missing? What would I do differently? Do I need to throw this out and start fresh?" They are not defeated. They are curious. They have learned something valuable and they are willing to dump the whole pot if necessary.

This mindset shift changes everything. Fear transforms into experimentation. Uncertainty becomes creativity. The unknown becomes exciting rather than paralyzing. You don't need to master French cuisine overnight. You just need to start tasting. Try one meeting without a rigid agenda and adjust based on what the team needs. Experiment with solving that recurring problem from a completely different angle. Test whether your standard approach is still the right recipe.

Each adjustment teaches you something deeper than following instructions ever could. Over time, this willingness to taste and adapt creates instincts other leaders never develop. The Tinkerer isn't following someone else's recipe. They are creating dishes that didn't exist before they started cooking.

The Tinkerpocalypse

The Tinkerer doesn't experiment in isolation. They don't tinker quietly in a corner, keeping their experiments to themselves, hoping no one notices they're trying something new. That's not how transformation happens.

The Tinkerer tinkers out loud and in doing so, they ignite something in everyone around them, energetic curiosity. Not the exhausting kind of curiosity that demands answers immediately or the performative kind that asks questions but doesn't really want to explore. The real kind, the alive kind. The kind that makes people lean in instead of check out. This is how individual tinkering becomes cultural transformation.

How do we improve patient satisfaction scores? We have tried everything. The team is stuck. They've been wrestling with the same problem for months. The energy is flat. People are going through the motions, proposing the same solutions that didn't work last time, hoping somehow this time will be different. And then the Tinkerer walks into a room. They simply ask questions; Why? How? What if? What happens next is magical. Instead of defending or deflecting, the team is now thinking. This is the spark. The spark that ignites the curiosity within the team; fueling the Tinkerer within.

What ignites this curiosity? Perhaps it is the Tinkerer's ability to bring spirited energy to problems. The kind of energy a kid brings to building with blocks. Trying this configuration. Knocking it down. Trying another. No shame when it falls. Just curiosity about what works. When a Tinkerer faces a serious challenge, they don't carry it like a burden. They carry it like an interesting puzzle.

There's lightness in the approach. Not lightness about the importance, but lightness about the permission to experiment. It gives people permission to suggest wild ideas without fear of being shot down. It makes it safe to try something that might not work. It transforms the culture from "we must execute perfectly" to "let's discover what works."

Igniting the Spark

Lead With Your Own Failed Experiments. Start meetings by sharing: "Here's something I tried this week that completely flopped. Here's what I learned." Your vulnerability gives permission. When the leader admits they're experimenting and failing, the team feels safe to do the same. The lightness comes from your modeling that failure isn't terminal. Be specific: Not "I made a mistake." But "I tried this new approach to staffing ratios and it created more problems than it solved. So now I'm trying this instead."

Celebrate the "Good Fail" at team huddles or meetings, ask: "Who tried something this week that didn't work but taught us something valuable?" Make it a regular practice. Publicly celebrate the person who experimented and learned, not just the person who succeeded. This rewires the culture from "don't mess up" to "learn something." Give it a name: "This week's Discovery Award" or "Best Learning Moment." Make the recognition visible. When people see experiments celebrated, they start offering them.

Establish the Two-Week Rule for any new approach: "We are trying this for two weeks. Then we assess. It might stay, it might go, it might morph into something else." The time boundary creates lightness. Nothing is permanent. Nothing is precious. Everything is an experiment with a built-in reflection point. This removes the weight of "getting it right forever."

When the Spark Becomes a Fire

A lot of leaders think they need to project certainty and have all the answers. Appear confident and in control at all times. The Tinkerer knows that's not just unnecessary, it's actually harmful.

Here's the secret weapon of the Tinkerer: they admit they don't know. Out loud for everyone to hear. In fact, they know when you pretend to have all the answers, you kill curiosity. Why would anyone explore alternatives if the leader already knows the right answer? Why would anyone experiment if the path is already decided?

It begins with vulnerability. When the team sees their leader willing to not know, willing to experiment, willing to learn from failure they allow themselves to do the same. In fact, vulnerability isn't weakness. It is the spark that ignites everyone else's courage.

Over time, the Tinkerer's energizing curiosity compounds into something bigger: a culture of tinkering. It starts with the Tinkerer asking curious questions, running visible experiments, and celebrating learning. Then a few brave souls try their own experiments. The Tinkerer celebrates those publicly. Then a few more people join in. Curiosity spreads. Tinkering becomes normal. Eventually, it's not just the leader tinkering. It's the whole team.

The culture has transformed. Not because of a mandate or a policy change. But because the Tinkerer's energizing curiosity was so contagious, so genuine, so rewarding that everyone wanted to be part of it. This is how one Tinkerer becomes a team of Tinkerers. This is how individual experiments become organizational transformation. This is how the spark becomes a fire.

CHAPTER NINE

Tinkerer Tenets

Denise Nelson Nash

Tinkering is like learning to ride a bike — being resourceful when faced with constraints, remaining curious, finding comfort in iterating and experimenting, and viewing a setback as an opportunity to exercise a growth mindset.

Tinkerer Tenets

As kids, we were encouraged to understand how things work. Often, it was in direct response to "I'm bored" or "What should we do now?" This meant challenging us to disassemble an object to understand its parts — to explore, discover, reveal, and understand the inner workings of things. Our adult guides aimed to spark our curiosity about how an object differs when viewed from the outside and the inside, and simply how things work. Building on the curiosity of objects, our adult guides then turned to our thinking processes. This sometimes meant taking what we had learned and seeing how combining words or concepts could create something new and wonderful. When we succeeded, and somehow, we always did, it was a delight to our young selves. In that moment, we embraced our newfound identities as explorers, scientists, engineers, and makers of things magical and wondrous.

Looking back, these childhood tinkering sessions prepared me for my leadership journey. The ability to recognize that not everything is as it appears. The willingness to experiment without knowing the outcome – to revisit, revise, and iterate. And to find comfort in discomfort with messy, sticky situations that could result in friction or solution-making. These weren't just childhood playtime; these were foundational leadership skills in the making. In today's complex and unpredictable world, the willingness to adapt and tinker is essential for navigating the ever-changing landscape of the leadership journey.

In The Art of Tinkering, authors Karen Wilkinson, Mike Petrich, and the Exploratorium celebrate what it means to tinker and be a Tinkerer — "the art of composing and decomposing physical things." In discovering this book, a flood of childhood memories returned. As a leader, considering what it means to tinker, the tinkering tenets outlined in the book resonated with me in terms of how they apply to a leader's experimentation, discovery, innovation, and inspiration—giving credit to the authors and perhaps apologies, as I adapt their tinkering tenets to serve as inspiration in engaging with the leadership journey.

Tinkerer Tenets
Not everything is as it appears

"Don't judge a book by its cover" is one of those proverbs that many of us learned early on in our lives and careers. This suggests that forming an opinion or judging something by its appearance or what can be seen can be deceptive. I invite you to join me in the memory of two situations that led me to be a Tinkerer at heart.

The Wearer of the Suit (The Great Man Theory)

Titles matter, right? Positionality matters, right? Years of experience matter, right? HE entered the room with the confidence of title, positionality, and experience. I immediately felt smaller, less than, and ready to assume a subservient role. In that moment, I was a child again, awed by the imposing figure in the tailored suit — the image of what society has taught us a leader should look like. As HE positioned himself in a physical posture of authority, the room fell silent with anticipation - something profound was about to happen. It could be words of wisdom or something truly innovative that only HE could conjure up. What happened next was perplexing. HE rambled, made pronouncements without evidence, and then invited questions.

This is a mindset tinkering story. It's one I have reflected on many times over the years. I continue to marvel at how societal conditioning creeps into our leadership journeys, no matter what our level of experience. At various points in our journey, we may find ourselves cascading down the waterfall to the pool of commonly accepted beliefs. The story of the wearer of the suit is emblematic of the unconscious bias each of us encounters along our journey.

It could be words of wisdom or something truly innovative that only HE could conjure up. What happened next was perplexing. HE rambled, made pronouncements without evidence, and then invited questions.

HIS ramblings took the form of making assumptions and stating his solutions to non-existent issues or perhaps issues from his previous role now mapped onto the new one. HE went on a long monologue about the issue, when HE obviously was not familiar with the data. Upon reflection, how would HE be as knowledgeable as those in the room after one month in the role. The average tenure of those in attendance was five years, with some having more than ten years of service. Then came the solutions to the non-existent problems without entertaining questions, querying for understanding, or showing some semblance of 'power with.' The solutions ricocheted around the room as HE listed one brilliant idea after another — brilliant to him. HE was so impressed with himself and his performance that he appeared unaware of the bewildered faces and shifting energy in the room. As he concluded HIS pronouncements, HE then asked for questions. Eyes darted around the room to confirm the shared experience. Heads bowed as text messages spun out into cyberspace and landed in the vibrating phones around the room. The silence that followed his pronouncements was not the reverence of wisdom, but the hush of expectations shattered. We sat in stillness like passengers on a train that stopped between stations, wondering if we were there yet.

Having enough recognition that HE had silenced the room after what felt like an eternity, although I wasn't sure if HE thought it was because he was so effective or there was recognition that HE lost the room, HE activated his number two. HIS number two shifted in their seat and conjured up as much confidence and diplomacy as they could. While doing their best to reinforce HIS carefully crafted presentation, the number two invited in the wisdom and experience of the room by acknowledging their expertise and asking for ways they might implement HIS recommendations. As politeness began peeling away, the room became vibrant with success stories and accounts of current and past efforts to address the areas HE identified. HE faded in the background. By the end of the 90 minutes, the room felt less in awe of HIM and more assured of their own competency. While HIS posture of self-assuredness didn't alter, the swiftness with which he departed was perhaps indicative of his own discomfort.

During HIS performance, I began to question and revise my initial assessment. It was time to tinker with my thoughts and draw upon my learning and thinking journeys. Like those childhood objects I learned to assemble and disassemble, this moment required me to examine the vertical lines of authority, the horizontal spaces of shared understanding, and the obtuse angles where appearance bows away from reality. Drawing a conclusion based on appearance and echoes of conditioning was a shared experience in the room. I had deceived myself into a belief that the person before me was going to impart some astounding insights. Was it the prototype leader image of the tall male in a tailored suit? Was it the air of assuredness HE entered the room with? Was it the title that preceded the delivery? Or perhaps a combination of all the above. What I know is that I failed myself. I failed to recognize the person before me and how I was responding to their presence. By this point in my leadership journey, I was considered an experienced leader. But even the most experienced leaders can fall prey to The Great Man Theory — the theory that certain men possess natural characteristics such as charm, superior intellect, courage, extraordinary leadership skills, and physical traits. I did. I let the imposter syndrome and insecurities in me surface — we all have them at one point or another. The feelings of not belonging and questioning if I was in the right space; the ones I thought were buried deep inside me surfaced; all these feelings and more bubbled up and pierced my balloon of assuredness. These foibles simmer under the surface of leadership, almost undetectable until a situation arises, and then it's the ah-ha moment that I, we, have been conditioned and must be ever vigilant. Thus, my reflection many times over the years to ensure I remain attentive to societal conditioning and remain steadfast in my beliefs and values.

And so, I steeled myself. Tapped into my resolve and removed the film through which I was seeing HIM to reveal the vacuous performance before me. The person who had attempted to embody The Great Man Theory and probably believed it until the bubble burst and the room saw him for what he was, the wearer of the suit. The image of the leader parts of society would have us believe is the prototype. What I discovered in that windowless conference room was not his inadequacy, but my own willingness to surrender my power to an image, a suit, a performance of leadership that echoed conditioning more than competence. What this revealed was about perception and the human tendency to create hierarchies. We construct hierarchies, much like children building sandcastles, which can be impressive from a distance but ultimately fragile, as we need to believe in them. None of us are immune to the allure of perceived power. We give away our power by empowering others based on a construct of apparent authority. But who decides who has authority over or power over?

Now, when I enter spaces where AUTHORITY presents itself in familiar forms, I pause. I disassemble what I see into its parts – the person, the position, the performance, the projection.

I tinker with my assumptions the way I once tinkered with non-functioning objects as a child, curious about what lies inside the exterior and patient enough to discover what is actually before me.

The figure behind a desk adorned with diplomas, credentials, and framed photos with recognizable public figures. The deliberate arrangement of furniture — an executive chair, two smaller guest chairs facing it. A voice of practiced confidence, sometimes wrapped in a literal uniform. The conversation that directs and decides while appearing to invite differing perspectives.

The person. Just a person, not a superior being. Someone who has doubts, fears, and uncertainties. Someone who maybe didn't sleep well the night before. Someone who might be having a bad day, like we all do. Not an authority on my worth.

The position. The structure within an organization that provides a title and power within a hierarchy. They occupy the seat temporarily. They may have access I don't, but it won't last forever. It's worth respecting, but it's not who they are. Who I am will not change with a title.

The performance. It's a craft honed by those who covet the influence that comes with a position. The way authority is enacted within a space, staged, and signaled to others. I've come to see this — sometimes well-practiced, sometimes clumsy, sometimes amusing — as individuals performing a version of themselves, they've rehearsed until it feels like skin. The performance wants me to see it as natural, effortless. It's not.

The projection. This is the difficult layer. Some of it is theirs — what they project onto me, their assumptions crafted based on their position and mine. But more of it is mine, what I give up to them from my own history, my own conditioning to defer, to shrink, to seek approval. I meet the present through the fog of my past, and I give them power they didn't have to ask for, that is only mine to own or surrender.

When I disassemble like this and see — really see — something shifts inside me. Confidence grows. Clarity arrives. And the authority before me shrinks to lowercase letters. I recapture my power. This is not disrespect for what AUTHORITY has achieved. This is me refusing to abandon myself in its presence.

Tinkerer Tenet: Leaning into Discomfort

"A bend in the road is not the end of the road unless you fail to make the turn."

Who hasn't experienced friction in their daily lives? Friction is all around us. Friction requires us to slow down and consider assumptions and details we encounter. Like a Tinkerer who explores how parts are connected before making adjustments, friction makes us pause to understand what's before us before acting. Friction can also be bad when it prevents progress through obstacles, delays, and distractions.

Throughout my journey, I have learned to embrace friction as a Tinkerer. I adjust, calibrate, and fine-tune when situations arise, believing that with the right combination of pause, patience, and reflection, situations can be improved. I approach leadership challenges like a plant mama - repotting when the roots are densely packed, pruning, cutting off shoots to encourage new growth, adjusting the location of a pot to improve the conditions for growth. The tinkering is gentle but intentional — seeing what thrives, what withers, and what needs to be changed. This instinct to tinker, adjust, and to fix has served me well. But what happens when the plant needs something you can't give it? What happens when your tinkering becomes the problem and not the solution? As you will read next my identity as a tinkerer was tested in ways I didn't anticipate.

Fixer Identity

Some people covet a leadership role, not fully understanding what the role entails and requires. During my leadership journey, I have encountered leadership in various forms. What I have come to know is that some costume themselves in what appears to be confidence and engage in performances of authority and competence. The unraveling follows.

Day one, the costume was confusing — after all, our first impressions are based on how one presents themselves within context. Instead of the professional, approachable attire that projects the responsibility of their role, the Ranking Executive arrived in a relaxed, floral-patterned silhouette with sensible shoes and a floppy hat. This attire may not have been attention-worthy in another setting; however, the institution they had joined prized both intellectual rigor and visual representation. The dissonance began before a word was spoken.

The Ranking Executive exuded a folksy warmth. They greeted each of us by name, expressing their excitement for the new role and gratitude that we would be there to guide them and assist in their transition. We may have been too quick to judge based on appearance. But we soon learned that the expressions of enthusiasm and openness to our guidance were all performative. The Ranking Executive was parroting all the words that one would expect from a new executive leader. Not long after the pageantry of arrival and pronouncements of collaboration and openness to learn had concluded, the friction began.

First, I tried small adjustments like providing guidance on cultural norms that would make their transition smoother, which was emphatically rejected with the fury that emerged from an unseen depth. It was the kind of tinkering I had done with other leaders to smooth the transition. What just happened to the folksy warmness?! Then, it was more substantial issues, such as providing background information and meeting preparation. I tinkered with my approach, adjusting my tone, the timing for offering advice or suggestions, and trying different tools from my toolkit. Leaders have to be agile and ready for the unexpected, but when this occurred with the Ranking Executive, it turned into a full-blown explosion of accusations of sabotage. After several of these encounters, I found myself suspended between compassion and self-preservation, witnessing my own faith in their leadership fade away like daylight into night.

I then began to question myself — was I the problem? Were my attempts to help somehow creating the obstacles I sought to remove? I slowed down, but I stalled on what to do next. I had made small adjustments to avoid raising their ire, but to no avail. It was then that I recognized I was viewing the problem through the wrong lens. Instead of focusing on the Ranking Executive's shortcomings, I needed to look inward. Recognizing my own attachment to being a "fixer," to being the one who would smooth rough edges and build connections, led me to reconsider my assumptions and gain a better understanding. I was so busy attempting to mend and fix that I didn't pause to recognize that friction was trying to teach me about my own limits of tinkering. Sometimes clarity comes when you step away and trust that not every rough edge requires your attention or can be smoothed out. In this case, friction was serving a purpose. It served the purpose of forcing me to stop to consider the information before me that I hadn't been ready to receive. To recognize that certain situations require different tools.

As an optimist and generative thinker, it's difficult, and there are times when everything points to tinkering is no longer working. Going in circles is one sign. Trying repeatedly, but the problem keeps returning. Things don't get better; they get worse. Not only does the problem keep returning, but it's like compound interest on an investment; there's more. You can't figure out why things aren't working. You can't explain it. That's another sign tinkering isn't working. When frustration sets in and curiosity wanes, the storyline is lost. When one or more of these persist, it's a signal that other tools are needed. This is particularly true in high-stakes situations where failure has reverberating consequences—time for first principles. Break the problem down into component parts and explore other options - read manuals, review tutorials, use planning tools, reverse engineering research, or consult with experts or trusted colleagues. This is where I landed.

I, the fixer, the Tinkerer, turned to others for help. Humility is often an underrated aspect of the leadership journey. There are times when one gets stuck, and to get unstuck, one needs the help of others. This was one of those situations, and my network of support was there for me. Having trusted confidants who understood the situation and viewed it through different vantage points was invaluable. The trusted confidants guided me with the same good intentions as I attempted to guide the ranking executive. Their wisdom around the need for me to let go of expectations and find comfort in viewing this setback in my leadership journey was an opportunity to exercise a growth mindset, and it was welcome. I came to realize what every plant mama learns: sometimes you've repotted, used the right soil, adjusted the amount of water and sunlight, and the plant still struggles. It's not because you failed, but some plants need what you can't give. Sometimes it's that the plant needs a different gardener. And in this, I realize that sometimes the bravest and most effective thing a Tinkerer can do is to put down the tools and stop tinkering. Not everything can be fixed.

CHAPTER TEN

The Tinkerer's Path

Lucas Welter

The Pace

Lucas walked fast. Not the forced hurry of someone late, but the natural speed of a mind in motion. His feet kept rhythm with his thoughts, and both moved quickly.

The AI device bounced against his chest as he moved. He tapped it while talking, his external brain, he said. For capturing ideas that came too fast to write down.

He talked about who we are as leaders versus who we want to be. About the gap between intention and action. How real transformation happens, not in boardrooms with strategic plans, but in small moments of honest reckoning. The insights arrived without warning, direct and urgent, delivered at walking speed. His energy built as the ideas formed; voice faster, steps faster, everything accelerating toward the venue ahead.

The topics tumbled out as we dodged tourists and students, his pace never slowing. His hands carved shapes in the air between sentences, building invisible architecture around each idea. In that motion, I realized he was the living embodiment of a Chief Catalyst: the spark that causes the reaction in everyone else. I could feel the electricity transferring to me, my own thoughts racing to match his cadence. With each question I asked, the reaction intensified his energy growing greater, growing stronger.

The door opened. Someone called his name. Before he turned, I pointed at the device. Did it capture all this? Lucas looked down, checked the light. Dark. He laughed., "I forgot to turn it on."

We stood there in the doorway; his whole rapid mind suspended for a moment. All those fast-moving ideas, unrecorded. The conversation had happened at the speed of his walking, at the speed of his brilliance, too quick to capture. Which was somehow exactly right.

-Trisha Beck

The work gets better because
the people get braver.

What If We're Preparing for the Wrong Test?

Becoming a leader is intentional work, but it's also slow-cooked—more blueprint-in-pencil than lightning bolt. You don't "arrive;" you iterate. Start with a simple purpose (who you serve and why), translate it into a few humble behaviors, and test them gently in the wild: ask "Tell me more," run the smallest useful experiment, set a decision clock. Expect wobble. Skills compound over seasons, not weekends, and most growth looks suspiciously like repetition. Invite feedback—mentors, peers, the colleague who tells you the truth—and treat it as design input, not a verdict. Keep a tiny log of wins and misses; celebrate progress the size of a Post-it. When you overreach, apologize; when you don't know, say so; when you learn, share it. Celebrate the people that help you grow. Leadership isn't a title or a personality type—it's a practice you keep showing up for, with curiosity, patience, and a willingness to redraw the map. Design the path, walk it, adjust. Time will do its part. People around you will notice.

Tinkering is a leadership approach that treats progress like a series of small, honest experiments: choose a direction, run the smallest useful test, watch what reality says back, and adjust—generously, publicly, and with others. It's bias-to-learning over bias-to-ego. Tinkering swaps the myth of the master plan for decision clocks, reversible moves when possible, and hypotheses instead of hunches. It's humble (we won't nail it on the first try), practical (ship a slice, not a saga), and human (safety to try beats pressure to perform). In short: design the path, walk it, listen, iterate. The work gets better because the people get braver.

I have one ambitious—maybe a little selfish —goal for this chapter: to give you everything I've learned. I want to take two decades of reflections, experiments, and idea-recombining and turn them into something you can actually use: an organized and actionable guide to choosing the tinkerer's path. Not with certainty. With seven **dispositions*** I keep returning to—testing, refining, and updating as I learn. Not rules. Just breadcrumbs. If they help you connect your own future dots, all the better: (1) Questions over answers fuel what to test next (2) Reflection doesn't have to be quiet (3) Everything is true—and so is its opposite (4) Cultures whisper before they shout (5) Assemble co-conspirators who will challenge and implement (6) Label it the Rotten First Draft and appoint a Chief Debunker (7) Prioritize courageous hunches over certainty. That's tinkering as leadership: curiosity with a backbone, humility with a cadence, and action that teaches. Now take these seven breadcrumbs, pocket them, and let's start building your next experiment—together, on purpose. The Disposition

*A few words about dispositions—especially if this is your first time hearing the term. (It was mine not long ago, thanks to Harvard's Project Zero—mysteriously named, and quietly one of the most influential voices on how learning actually happens, especially through the arts.)

Dispositions are the quiet engine under leadership because they blend inclination, sensitivity, and ability. Take reflective leadership: you need the will to reflect (inclination), the radar to notice the moment worth reflecting on (sensitivity), and the method to do it without turning your week into a diary of doom (ability). Miss one, and you wobble—well-intentioned but clumsy, skilled but oblivious, or hyper-aware and stuck.

Skills get tasks done. Dispositions decide how and why you show up to do them. You can teach anyone to run a meeting (skill). Whether they listen, invite dissent, adapt, or bulldoze? That's disposition—and that's what people remember.

Here's why this matters: dispositions travel. They show up in the high-stakes meeting and in Tuesday's email thread. They're also teachable (good news), and they compound over time. When we call someone "curious" or "compassionate," we're pointing to how they habitually meet the world—not just what they know.

Skills can expire. Dispositions evolve. You can relearn a spreadsheet. It's harder (and more valuable) to cultivate persistence, curiosity, generosity, or courage—the operating system that helps every new skill load faster.

So yes: build skills. But nurture dispositions. They're your renewable edge—the part of you people trust when there's no map—and the reason they'll follow you while you draw one.

Here are my seven dispositions for tinkering as a leadership journey.

1. Questions Are Better Than Answers

Leadership begins the moment you choose curiosity over certainty. Answers feel satisfying—like closing a tab. Questions, though, open three new tabs and invite other people to click. That's the point: leadership isn't a solo act; it's a browser with many contributors.

When I was five, the year before school started—this was in a world (and a country) where kindergarten began at six and formal literacy at seven—my mother read to me of each story, she'd pause and ask me to invent a different ending, or to wonder why the hero's shirt was blue and not orange (nothing is more contagious than the childlike sense of wonder). It was never about getting it "right." It was about looking again. "What else?" became a default setting in my brain, a little mental lever that pries open new perspectives. Those bedtime edits were an early apprenticeship in leadership: not the power to answer, but the permission to ask.

Years later, my favorite leadership phrase is still "Tell me more." Not because I'm short on ideas (I carry them around like carry-on luggage), but because the best insights usually belong to the person across from me. Curiosity creates space; space builds trust; trust gets things moving. Answers can shut a conversation down. Questions stretch the horizon.

Confession: I'm a natural converger. I like to find the path forward and start walking. I was also educated in an era that prized knowing things and then knowing to do things. I could recall facts, connect dots, and—back when our phones didn't store the accumulated knowledge of humankind—be very "useful." Useful, yes. Inspiring? Not always. Playing the answer machine puts you in a power position and reduces everyone else to spectators. Later, I was lucky to ride the wave of "teaching for understanding"—the habit of asking why something works, what causes it, and where it breaks. That shift made questioning second nature.

We've all survived the "Smartest Person in the Room" meeting—our Great Wearer of the Suit in peak form—and it's a sport with no winners—and the real cost is that the best contributions (the clarifying, beginner-minded questions) never make it into the air.

Questions are not a tactic to delay decisions. They're how we make better ones. The right questions expand the circle of voices, reveal the edges of our blind spots, and light up the system we're operating in. Systems thinking begins with inquiry: What are the incentives? What are the constraints? Where are the bottlenecks? Who benefits, who bears the cost, and who's missing from this conversation? Good questions rescue us from false certainty and expensive rework later.

Even "I don't know" can be a high-trust move. Said honestly, it signals respect for reality and for your team. It opens the floor to evidence, not ego. In fast-moving environments, humility is not a personality trait—it's a risk-management strategy.

The first time "Tell me more" escaped my mouth, it was an accident—an elegant way of saying I had no idea what to ask next. As someone born and raised in Brazil, I learned early that privacy is an elastic concept—the border between "personal" and "personal-ish" is drawn in pencil. But here I was in a different cultural context, wondering: Where's the line on this map? How do I be exactly the right amount of 'curious' without unintentionally crossing the line?

So I tried a small experiment. For everything I wanted to know but didn't want to bulldoze, I offered three words: "Tell me more." It became my consent-based curiosity. She decided how far to go; I followed at her pace. No genius involved—just a question that changed the frame. Somewhere over the Rockies I understood: leadership isn't the authority to answer; it's the courage to inquire, to make room for someone else's story to land.

Now, the honest trade-off: living by questions means making friends with unfinished sentences. Inquiry creates productive tension—more possibilities, more perspectives, and, yes, more ambiguity. Expect moments without closure. Curiosity is the extra set of headlights on a dark road—it lets you see farther before you commit to the turn. Leading with questions will not deliver permanent closure, but it will deliver continuous clarity. You trade the illusion of certainty for the reality of progress.

The leadership journey doesn't begin when someone gives you a title or a microphone. It begins when you replace certainty with curiosity, competition with exploration, and performance with learning. Ask better questions, and you don't just get better answers—you get better teams, better decisions, and, quietly, a better you. "Tell me more" is not a soft move. It's strategy, it's culture, and it's how real change actually starts.

If you want a place to start this week, here are some tactics for you:
- "What would have to be true for this to work?" (Opens possibilities without hand-waving.)
- "Who else is impacted and not in the room?" (Invites the system to speak, my favorite definition of diversity: who is not in the room?)
- "What is the smallest useful test we could run?" (Converts debate into learning.)

And maybe add one more, in honor of those childhood rewrites: "What else?" It's small, generous, and relentless. Ask it, and watch the story change.

2. Reflection Doesn't Have to Be Quiet

I don't sit cross-legged in candlelight. I pace. I talk. I leave myself voice notes from grocery aisles and airport gates. That's my reflection—mobile, chatty, a little chaotic—and it works. Reflection isn't a yoga pose; it's a practice of noticing. Leaders don't need silence; we need sense-making.

My apprenticeship started in a bright Brazilian bathroom. Lunch was the main meal; school happened in shifts; and between the two, my mother (who was a lawyer but initially trained as a primary school teacher) sat at her vanity for twenty quiet minutes, applying makeup and asking impossible questions. Next to the mirror there was a chair—the cadeira de pensar, the reflection chair. If one of us needed a nudge (or a reality check), she'd invite us to sit and then launch a guided reflection: "What did you hope would happen?" "What else might be true?" "If you were me, what would you do next?" Torturous then, priceless now. She didn't lecture; she coached our thinking out loud, modeling that reflection is a conversation with consequences. The chair taught me that accountability can be loving and that questions, delivered calmly, rearrange a pre-teenager's brain faster than any punishment ever could.

Fast-forward to my own leadership rituals: the Wall of Sticky Notes. Before remote work turned our walls into Zoom backgrounds, I'd paper mine with neon thoughts—assumptions, options, half-baked sketches. Colleagues knew the wall was communal. Add, move, cross out. Don't ask permission; make it better. People would stop by and leave a question mark next to a risky idea or draw an arrow between two notes I hadn't connected. I'd return from a meeting and discover that my thinking had evolved without me. That's the magic of making learning visible: you convert private processing into social clay everyone can shape. You also de-dramatize iteration. A crossed-out Post-it isn't failure; it's progress you can compost. Ask anyone at AFS about Lucas and I bet the first answer will be sticky notes.

Learning is happening all the time. But if no one can see it—not even you—how do you build on it?

Somewhere along the way, we confused "reflective" with "quiet." But reflection is less posture than posture-taking: a stance of curiosity toward our own patterns. Speak it, sketch it, map it, meme it—just get it out of your head and into a shared space where others can build on it. When leaders show their work—messy drafts, decision logs, "why we changed our mind" notes—we normalize adaptation. We teach that growth beats performance and that ideas, like cities, improve through public use.

So let's make it visible. Sticky notes. Whiteboards. Debriefs. Bad drawings. Tangents. Whatever works. Just get the learning out of people's heads and into the shared space where it can breathe. That's where real progress lives.

If you want a place to start this week, try these:

- Pick a chair. What's your *cadeira de pensar* ritual? Ten minutes, one question: What did I intend? What actually happened? What will I try next?
- Show your wall. What's one decision you can "post-it in public"—assumptions, options, next test—so others can add, question, or connect?
- Narrate the change. After your next adjustment, how will you share a five-sentence "lab note" (signal seen, decision made, next test) so the team learns with you?

3. Everything Is True—and So Is Its Opposite

One of leadership's most useful (and mildly annoying) truths: two contradictory things can both be right—depending on context, timing, and who's in the room. Transparency builds trust... until it floods people with unfinished thinking and breeds anxiety. Structure unlocks clarity... until it cages creativity. Speed delights... until it breaks quality. The point isn't to pick a side and write it on your values wall. The point is to learn the dance. Nuance isn't dithering; it's a discipline. And yes, people can smell the difference.

Years ago, I bought a wall clock that ran counterclockwise and hung it in my office. (Guests hated it. Time should not moonwalk, they said. But they were puzzled by the idea.) That little rebellion was my daily nudge: we designed everything around us; therefore, we can redesign it. If clockwise is "true," then, under certain conditions, its opposite can be true enough to be useful. The clock made my brain stumble—then look again. It also sparked hallway conversations: "Why is your clock wrong?" Perfect opening. "Maybe the question is: when does our default run the wrong way?" That clock now lives with a dear friend in Italy, confusing and educating another set of visitors. Best souvenir I've ever exported: an invitation to interrogate assumptions.

Here's the leadership move: stop treating paradoxes as puzzles to "solve" and start treating them as systems to steer. You don't resolve a paradox—you manage it.

Most tensions live between *two good things*. So the job is to name the tension, set a few guardrails, and run small, reversible tests. Instead of declaring "We are a transparency-first org," try something designed for reality: "We share early drafts by default inside the team; we share decisions by default outside the team." Same value. Better steering.

And remember: people rarely resist change because they hate the future. They resist because they're unsure where they fit in it. The strategy can be solid—and someone's role can suddenly feel fuzzier. Your job is to draw the map (yes, literally): what stays, what changes, and where experiments live. Partial clarity beats counterfeit certainty every day of the week.

Tinkering makes this practical. Hold two truths without getting whiplash: write two hypotheses that contradict each other, test both, learn fast, adjust without drama. That's not moral relativism—it's contextual intelligence. And it's how teams get braver: complexity is allowed, and it's navigable. If you want a place to start this week, try these:

- Name the tension. On one page, write the pair you're wrestling (e.g., Structure ↔ Creativity). Under each side, list "wins when…" conditions. What boundary keeps each side healthy?
- Run the duel. Frame two opposing micro-tests with success signals and a 2-week decision clock. What will we see if A works better than B?
- Map the humans. For your current change, sketch three columns: What stays the same / What changes / What we'll protect while we learn. Who gains clarity from this map today?

4. Cultures Whisper Before They Shout

The first time I misread a meeting room in another culture, I was sure I'd broken something important. (Spoiler: I hadn't. Maybe dented it. It felt like a demolition.) Culture rarely arrives with a bullhorn. It's a whisper: a seat that stays empty for a reason, a pause that means "I'm thinking" not "I'm done," an agenda item that isn't on the agenda but is definitely in the room. When you cross countries, teams, or sectors, the only reliable tool is humility. Enter curious—not neutral, curious. Neutral observes; curiosity inquires.

My apprenticeship in culture really started when I was elected president of the student association in architecture school, and I arrived with a righteous plan: streamline what was bureaucracy to me, reduce the endless discussions, and get to work. I wanted action; the association prized process. We'd sit through three-hour debates to ensure every voice was heard and consensus actually meant something. To me, it felt like molasses. After three months, I was exhausted and secretly judging the whole ritual as a performative delay.

Then my methods failed—spectacularly. People complied, but nothing moved. My mistake? I tried to change the dance without learning the steps. When I finally shut up and watched, a different pattern emerged. Those "tedious" debates were guardrails. They distributed ownership. They filtered out brittle ideas. They made sure that when we did act, we acted together. I stopped bulldozing, started listening, honored the established norms—and then nudged them. We shortened rounds, assigned rotating facilitators, and moved from "consensus or bust" to "consent to try." The association got faster because it didn't feel hijacked. Only later, meeting Charles Handy and Edgar Schein on the page, did I have language for what I'd lived: culture is the set of assumptions that teach us what's safe, what's smart, and what's sacred. If you ignore it, it will ignore you back.

Years later, in that foreign meeting room, I recognized the same trap. My instinct was to fill the silence. In that context, silence meant respect and signal-seeking, not confusion. I was reading with my own alphabet. So I switched to presence over prescriptions. I asked a local colleague to co-facilitate, mirrored their pacing, and moved decisions into reversible pilots. The temperature dropped; participation rose. No heroics—just small acts of cultural humility repeated until trust showed up.

Here's the practice that keeps saving me: Listen for the whispers. What gets praised? What gets punished? Who speaks first? Who never interrupts whom? Which agenda item always runs out of time? The answers map the real operating system. Change sticks when your tests align with (or gently stretch) those underlying assumptions. This is tinkering with presence: watch → name → nudge. Watch the patterns without drama. Name them aloud, lightly and specifically. Nudge with the smallest useful test, designed to be safe in this culture, not an imaginary neutral one.

And when—not if—you misstep, repair fast and clean. "I moved too quickly for our norm of consultation. Here's what I learned. Here's how

I'll adjust next time." Repair is not weakness; it's cultural competence. Communities forgive honest mistakes; they remember defensive ones. Culture is patient—but it does keep score.

Leadership across cultures isn't an etiquette checklist; it's attentiveness with a backbone. Can you notice what you weren't trained to notice? Can you honor what's sacred and suggest a reversible way to try something new? The bolder the change, the quieter the entry. Start by paying attention. Then keep going.

If you want a place to start this week, try these:

- Borrow Local Eyes (perhaps the most important advice I was given in life). Pair with a cultural insider (country, department, or generation). Ask: What am I not seeing? When do we move too fast? When do we move too slow? Co-design a micro-test that honors one norm while stretching another.
- Practice Clean Repair. Draft a four-sentence template you can use on repeat: What I did; the norm I bumped; what I learned; what I'll do differently next time. Who needs that note from you this week—before the whisper becomes a shout?

5. Assemble Co-Conspirators Who Will Challenge and Implement

If your leadership only works when you're on top, it's not leadership— it's a one-person show with a tired audience. The best decisions I've made came from people who had zero incentive to please me and every incentive to tell me the truth. Tinkering is a team sport. You assemble a circle of folks brave enough to disagree with you—and practical enough to build the next version with you. Circles aren't symbolic; they're practical. No one sits too far from the center. Ideas move faster. Accountability is shared. Towers feel safe; circles create momentum.

Many moons ago, I was facilitating a very tense three-day meeting in India—about 120 people, months of heat in the system, everyone ready to make grand speeches. I opened with a procedural softball: "Shall we approve the agenda?" The room said no. The air left my lungs for exactly ten seconds. I admitted I was stuck (out loud), jogged to the back, and asked my co-facilitator, Carolyn, for a lifeline. She smiled like a Jedi and said, "Small circles." The Montessori kid that I am, the geometry made instant sense. We ditched the podium, formed groups of six, and gave a simple sequence: write alone, pair up, then share in your small circle before returning to the whole. The temperature dropped; wisdom surfaced. Positions softened because people heard themselves think—and each other think. By afternoon, we had a short list of reversible tests everyone could live with. That day, the shape of the room did half the facilitation.

How do you build your circle? Start with character, not charisma: kind, direct humans who ship things. You're looking for people who can do both parts of the job—challenge the thinking and implement the next test. Invite the builder who turns decisions into drafts, the skeptic who pressure-tests assumptions, the connector who braids perspectives, and the scribe who makes learning visible so the system can remember. Make disagreement a service, not a performance. Give the circle a cadence (decision clocks, short write-ups, the next small test) and a norm: we argue to improve the work—then we move. Followers are optional. Co-conspirators are non-negotiable: people who give a damn and make the work better because they refuse to let it stay theoretical. A circle won't save you from hard calls, but it will save you from lonely, brittle ones. The work gets better because the people get braver—together.

And remember to celebrate your co-conspirators. No, celebrating people isn't fluffy. It's infrastructure—the fuel that keeps a truth-telling, action-taking circle intact. Two years ago, at the start of a workshop with thirty young participants from twelve Asian countries, we opened with simple pair introductions. While they spoke, a thought kept buzzing: in the social enterprise world, young adults do astonishing things while carrying a heavy backpack labeled impostor syndrome. The question: how do we help lighten it—fast? The answer arrived after the first introduction. Celebrate more. Celebrate now. I grabbed a flip chart and, for each person, wrote one or more concrete things we could honor—clarity in values, persistence with a community project, kindness shown to a teammate. Two hours later the walls were covered with a mural of "small and big things to celebrate." The energy spike was visible. People sat taller. Over three days, the room kept returning to those pages, harvesting courage from evidence already in the system. Celebration didn't distract from the work; it supercharged it—because brave people iterate faster.

If you want a place to start this week, try these:

- Change the shape. In your next meeting, run this 15-minute sequence: 2 minutes solo notes → 5 minutes pairs → 8 minutes in groups of 4–6 → 1 minute full-room headlines. What emerged that a tower would have crushed?
- Audit your tower. List three people who will tell you when you're wrong. Invite them into your next decision—and commit to acting on at least one of their suggestions.
- Monday Love / Friday Repair. Block 20 minutes each Monday to send three specific thank-yous. Block 20 on Friday to apologize or close a loop. Who needs to hear "I saw that" or "I'm sorry" from you this week?

6. Label it the Rotten First Draft—on purpose, in plain sight—and appoint a Chief Debunker.

Tinkering gets framed as dithering by people who mistake confidence for competence. The best leaders I know tinker relentlessly. Not because they lack a plan, but because they know progress is built from drafts. Tinkering is movement with humility: try something small, see what reality says back, adjust in public. Ship a slice, not a saga.

Why I often speak first in a meeting: not to anchor the room, but to de-risk it. I go first to model that our opening move is a prototype, not a proclamation. My first contribution is intentionally scrappy—90 seconds, one hypothesis, two ways I'm probably wrong, and a signal that would change my mind. The message is clear: "This is a draft. Make it better." When leaders treat their words like wet clay, others feel permission to put hands on the sculpture.

Yes, speaking first can backfire. Anchoring is real. The antidote is framing. I literally label my opener: "bad first draft," "strawman," or "consent-to-try." I attach a decision clock (though my cultural background allows me to be very flexible with time) and ask for disconfirming evidence first: "What would break if we shipped this?" You avoid groupthink by rewarding the person who finds the edge case, not the person who nods the loudest.

One of my teammates teases me: "Lucas loves to be proven wrong." Guilty—and strategic. Being publicly correct is nice; being publicly improvable is culture. When I float a half-idea, people who might stay quiet jump in. The builder adds a workable step. The skeptic finds the hidden cost. The operator names the dependency we forgot. Suddenly we have something real enough to test by Friday. That's tinkering: not debate club, build club.

You test something not because it's perfect, but because it's promising. You narrate what happened—signal seen, tweak made, next step—so learning sticks beyond the moment. We don't need more pundits; we need more builders. If you're waiting to be "ready," you're already late. Start small, start visible, start together.

If you want a place to start this week, try these:

- Lead with a prototype. Open one meeting with a 90-second strawman: hypothesis, smallest test, two ways it might fail, decision clock. Ask first for what would make you change your mind.
- Assign the breaker. Name one person "Chief Debunker" for each discussion. Their job is to find the edge case before it finds you. Rotate the role.
- Ship a slice by Friday. Pick one idea and deliver the tiniest usable version. Post a three-line lab note: what we tried, what we saw, what we'll adjust next. Repeat.

7. Prioritize Courageous Hunches Over Certainty

You don't need certainty to begin. You need a hunch that won't let you sleep, a value you're unwilling to trade away, a stake in the outcome—and the courage to place the first dot. Not privately, not perfectly—publicly, imperfectly. Because once the first dot is visible, it becomes an invitation. And invitations, repeated with care, are how movements start.

What if organizational change behaved less like a project plan and more like a movement? Movements don't begin with declarations; they begin with a felt gap—between what is and what could be—and one person deciding, I'm going to place the first dot. You rarely see the full picture in advance. You make a mark, then another, then another. Patterns appear. People join. The future is not delivered; it's drawn. Dot by dot.

Here's the unglamorous truth: movements scale through clarity and cadence, not charisma. A mic is optional. A manifesto is optional. What's non-optional is a small, visible practice others can copy without asking you for permission. Start with a tiny flag—one behavior, one ritual, one template—that quietly says, "This is who we are becoming." Keep it so lightweight that anyone can carry it into their Tuesday. My favorite "dot" is the public lab note. Years ago I posted a one-page update after a messy pilot—what we tried, what signal we saw, what we'd change next—no spin, just learning in daylight. The pilot had flopped in a very specific way: we designed a new process, trained people, and then watched it die in contact with reality because it asked for too much time, too much coordination, and too much permission. Participation dropped off after week one. Confusion spiked. A few people quietly reverted to the old way and pretended it was "temporary." In the lab note, I named the failure plainly: *our design was elegant; our adoption path was absurd.* I listed the assumptions that didn't hold, the friction points we underestimated, and the smallest next version we would test—plus one sentence I didn't love writing but needed to: *"This one is on me."* It cost me ten minutes and a bit of pride. Within a month, other teams were posting their own. No training. No mandate. Just a pattern that made sense and lowered the cost of entry. Movements spread when the next step is both obvious and doable.

You'll be tempted to centralize. Resist it. Movements need stewards more than bosses: people who hold the purpose steady, protect the tone, and multiply the number of places the work can live. Give away the tools—templates, stories, decision clocks—so others can adapt them locally. Celebrate replication over ownership. An idea is winning when you see it in the wild with someone else's fingerprints on it.

And please: tell a story where people can see themselves inside. Strategy maps inform; stories recruit. If your change narrative requires a cape and your exact job title, it won't travel. If it features ordinary Tuesdays, reversible tests, and neighbors who look like us, it will. Movements grow at the speed of belonging.

If you want a place to start this week, try these:

- Plant a tiny flag. What is one 10-minute ritual (lab note, wall of wins, consent-to-try) you can model publicly so others can copy it tomorrow?

- Create a commons. Where will the dots live—so anyone can add theirs without asking you? What's the simplest template that makes participation obvious?
- Recruit by story. Who's your "ordinary Tuesday" hero? How will you share their 90-second story so others think, That could be me—what dot can I add?

Don't Be Perfect, Be Brave

These breadcrumbs aren't definitive. They're evolving—iterating—like I am. Like we all are. But if anything in here rings true for you, take it. Use it. Change it. Share what you learn.

We don't need perfect leaders. We need brave ones. Thoughtful ones. Leaders who learn, think, and tinker their way into better futures—not just for themselves, but for everyone else too.

So pick one breadcrumb and run one small test this week. Let's leave good dots behind. Better yet—let's lay some ahead.

Connecting the Dots Forward

The dots you lay today become the path others follow tomorrow.

What if everything you know about leadership prepared you for the past?

Pause for a moment. Let the question land. Stay with how the question feels.

We asked you this question at the beginning of our journey together. Now, we want to answer it: Everything you have just learned prepares you for tomorrow.

Think back to where you were when you first opened this book. You have traveled with us through stories of failure and discovery. You have sat in the discomfort of not knowing. You have witnessed leaders who got it completely wrong and others who stumbled their way toward something right.

And here's what we invite you to recognize: this wasn't a straight line. Leadership growth rarely is. Like the rhythms of seasons, your learnings have their own pacing and cycles. Sometimes in rapid spurts, sometimes unfolding slowly, and other times barely perceptible transitions from one learning to another.

You have been invited to pause, to question, to experiment. And now you are different. Not finished, just different. Still becoming.

The Journey

The Learner taught you that leadership begins with humility. That "I don't know" can be the most powerful thing you say all day. That growing pains aren't signals to stop but instead invitations to expand. That discomfort is the price of admission for transformation. The Learner showed you how to break free from the Groundhog Day trap, to stop hoarding aged knowledge like an antique dealer, to resist the fatal flaw of needing all the answers. The Learner gave you permission to be human.

The Thinker showed you that action without reflection is just motion. That silence can be the most productive "sound" in a room. That the pause between question and answer is where wisdom lives. The Thinker taught you to create sanctuaries, both internal and external for genuine thought. To practice dolphin-thinking where collaboration is more powerful than individual brilliance, to make your thinking visible so others can build on it. The Thinker gave you permission to slow down.

The Tinkerer invited you to stop walking the well-worn path and start carving new canyons. To treat everything as a first draft worth improving. To experiment where people can see it, to fail forward, to adjust like a hummingbird, constantly, precisely, joyfully. The Tinkerer showed you that vulnerability isn't weakness but the doorway to innovation. That celebration is a strategy, not a ceremony. That movements begin with one person laying one dot. The Tinkerer gave you permission to try.

But here is what we hope you have discovered: These aren't separate roles you switch between. Instead they are a journey.

You learn something from a challenging experience. You create space to think about what it means. You tinker with a new approach. Then you learn from that experiment, think about what worked and what didn't, and tinker again. This is the Trinity journey.

The Learner asks the questions. The Thinker creates space for those questions to breathe. The Tinkerer experiments with answers. And the journey continues, each time with deeper wisdom and with greater impact.

The Landmarks: The Points of Connection

The Journey Never Ends

Learning, thinking, and tinkering have no end. The day you believe you have arrived is the day you stop leading. The highway continues, the growing pains never fully fade, the dance keeps evolving. The treasure isn't found at the destination; the treasure is the journey itself. Are you committed to the journey?

The Mystery of Readiness

Learning requires a state of readiness. What does that look like for you?

For you, readiness may have been when you opened this book. Or it might come next Tuesday, Wednesday, or Thursday, when a challenge or situation presents itself that looks familiar through your new lens. The mystery of readiness to learn and the mystery of openness is to be celebrated. This is about openness and curiosity — the readiness to learn, to receive, to see.

Be open and receptive to your own rhythm of growth. Give this to yourself.

Vulnerability as Fuel

The comfort of certainty is a trap. The vulnerability of not knowing is a superpower. Bravery and courage aren't the absence of fear; they are the willingness to move forward despite it. The learning happens in the uncomfortable space between not knowing and discovering. Between certainty and curiosity. Between the question and the answer. What discomfort are you avoiding, what growth are you missing?

Questions Over Answers

Questions expand knowledge; answers often stifle it. Questions illuminate blind spots and reveal assumptions. The learning leader asks; the performer answers. "Tell me more" creates space. "I don't know" builds trust. "What if?" opens possibilities. What questions will you ask tomorrow that you were afraid to ask today?

The Power of the Pause

Speed does not equal wisdom or decisiveness. The power of the pause creates clarity. Reflection fuels better action. Sometimes the most decisive thing a leader can do is deciding to learn more before deciding what to do. Embody reflection and thinking time as it is not a delay, it is due diligence. How will you find peace in the pause instead of filling every silence with noise?

Unlearning to Learn

What got you here won't get you there. Connect with your unconscious; challenge what you "know." Past experiences shape you, but they can also trap you. The antique leader curates the past. The learning leader architects the future. What are you ready to unlearn so I can learn what's needed now?

Humanity at the Center

Leadership is a human business, period. Learning, thinking, and tinkering are about human connection, not command and control. Mary Parker Follett's wisdom endures: power with rather than power over. Who will share your learning journey? Who will be your thought partner? Who will tinker alongside you? Who will you invite on this journey?

Your Trinity Journey: What is Next?

From the Learner

1. "Tell Me More": Ask "Tell me more." Especially when you think you already understand. Especially when you're ready to provide the answer. Notice what happens.

2. Growing Pains: Ask yourself: "What made me uncomfortable today?" Then ask the follow-up: "What was that discomfort trying to teach me?" Write it down. One sentence is enough. Watch for patterns.

3. The Strategic Disruptor: Choose one "we've always done it this way" pattern in your organization. Ask "Why?" five times. Not to be annoying, but to truly understand the layers. You might discover a good reason. You might discover there isn't one. Either way, you have learned something.

From the Thinker

1. The Sacred Pause Before responding, especially when you have the perfect answer ready, pause for five full seconds. Count them. Feel the discomfort. Notice what happens in that space.

2. Visible Thinking: Create a physical or digital space where you make your thinking visible. Use sticky notes, use a shared document, use whatever works. Post a problem you are working through. Add your thoughts as they evolve. Invite others to add theirs. Let it be messy.

3. Dolphin-Thinking; In your team meeting try this structure: Two minutes of silent individual thinking, five minutes in pairs, eight minutes in small groups, then only two minutes for the full group

to share key insights. Notice how the quality of thinking changes when you plan space for it.

From the Tinkerer

1. The Friday Experiment: Every Friday afternoon, try one new small thing. A different meeting format. A new way of giving feedback. An unfamiliar route to solve a familiar problem. Document what happened in three sentences. What did you try? What did you notice? What will you change?

2. The Public Prototype: Share one idea this week explicitly as a "bad first draft." Say those words out loud. "This is a bad first draft, and I would love your help making it better." Watch how it changes the conversation. Notice who speaks up.

3. The Celebration: Start your next meeting with: "What is one thing someone tried this week, whether it worked or not, that we should recognize?" Notice how this shifts the energy and the team's willingness to experiment.

The Moments that Matter

You might be asking yourself, when will I know I'm ready? How will I recognize the moments that matter?

The truth is you might not recognize them at the moment. Often, it will be upon reflection, in the rearview mirror. And that's okay. What matters is building the awareness muscle.

Here's what that might look like.

The moment someone asks you a question and you have the perfect answer ready. You will feel the pull to deliver it. To be smart, to be helpful, to move things along. That is the moment that matters. Will you give the answer, or will you pause and ask, "What do you think?" or

"Tell me more about the situation"? The first path is faster. The second path builds the thinker.

The moment a meeting feels stuck and uncomfortable. The silence is there. The tension will rise. You will want to fill the space, fix the problem, move past the discomfort. That is the moment that matters. Will you rush to resolution, or will you hold the pause long enough for someone else's thinking to emerge? The first path feels productive. The second path creates breakthroughs.

The moment someone proposes an idea that you are certain won't work. You will have data, experience, and logic on your side. You will want to explain why it's not a good idea. That is the moment that matters. Will you shut it down, or will you ask, "What's the smallest version of that we could test to learn?" The first path protects resources. The second path builds a tinkering culture.

The moment you make a mistake and people are watching. You will feel the urge to explain it away, minimize it, or point to external factors. That is the moment that matters. Will you defend, or will you own it cleanly and share what you learned? The first path protects your ego. The second path builds trust.

The moment you are asked to make a decision without enough information. The pressure will be real. People will be waiting. You will feel the expectation to be decisive, to act, to lead. That is the moment that matters. Will you make a call to appear confident, or will you say, "I need to think about this and gather more input, let's follow-up at [specific time]?" The first path looks like leadership. The second path is leadership.

These moments that matter will arrive quietly, without announcement. Often you won't recognize them until they have passed. That's okay. The journey is not about perfection; it's about direction. Over time, as you practice, you will catch these moments earlier. You will make different choices more often. You will course-correct faster when you don't.

The Trinity Impact

You notice different things. You catch yourself before you provide the answer someone else should discover. You sense when a meeting needs silence instead of more talking. You spot the moment when a decision should be reversible instead of permanent. Your awareness has expanded.

You feel different. The exhaustion of pretending to know everything has lifted. The pressure to always be right has eased. You are more curious than defensive. More playful than rigid. You actually enjoy Mondays again because each week brings new experiments, not just the same problems.

Most importantly, you are different. You are not the same leader who started this book. You have evolved and you are still evolving. You have made peace with the journey having no destination. You have embraced being permanently in beta test mode. You have discovered that leadership isn't about arrival instead it is about continuous becoming.

But it requires commitment. Not perfection, commitment. The commitment to choose learning when certainty feels safer. To choose thinking when action feels more urgent. To choose tinkering when the well-worn path beckons.

One year from now, when someone asks you, "How did you transform your leadership?" you won't point to a framework or a technique. You will tell them about the time you finally admitted you didn't know and how the room exhaled. You will describe the meeting where twenty seconds of silence changed everything. You will share the small experiment that failed but taught you something vital.

Similar is Not the Same

One of the fundamental mistakes often present in the leadership journey is assuming similar equals the same.

What worked in your previous role? Similar, not the same.

Who were you six months ago? Similar, not the same.

Knowing from past experiences can be helpful or it can blind us to what is before us.

The learning leader knows the difference. The Learner approaches situations with curiosity and openness about what makes this moment, this team, this challenge unique. There isn't a single moment of clarity, but a multi-layered unfolding to the complexity and beauty of leadership in real time.

The Movement

This journey is not just about you becoming a better leader. This is about transforming the systems around you. When you learn publicly, you give permission for others to be Learners. When you create thinking space, you normalize thinking. When you tinker visibly, you make experimentation safe. Your leadership creates pathways for others.

Michael's vulnerability about not knowing created space for his teams to admit the same. Trisha's twenty seconds of silence in a huddle surfaced critical patient information. Sharon's celebration culture turned the team of individual contributors into true collaborators. Herminio's self-compassion modeling freed others to value themselves. Denise's willingness to be the "newbie" taught teams that curiosity matters more than credentials. Lucas's public prototypes made it safe for entire organizations to try and iterate.

One Tinkerer becomes a team of Tinkerers. One Learner creates a learning culture. One Thinker's pause becomes an organization's rhythm. You are not just changing yourself. You are changing the force of your entire team. You see, each day you are teaching them what leadership looks like.

What are they learning? When you practice the Trinity, they learn that curiosity is valued. That thinking matters. That experimentation is expected. That vulnerability is strength. That learning never ends. And then the beautiful part, they start doing it too.

This is how individual transformation becomes cultural transformation. This is how one leader multiplies into many. This is how real change happens, through lived examples that others can follow. Your dots become their dots. You see, you are not just becoming the leader you want to be. You are becoming the leader others will learn from, whether you realize you're teaching or not.

The Promise

If you commit to the journey, if you practice being a Learner, a Thinker, and a Tinkerer with intention and consistency, you will transform. Not into some idealized version of a leader but instead into a more authentic, more effective, more human version of yourself.

You will make better decisions. You will build stronger teams. You will create more innovation. You will experience less burnout and more joy. But more than that, and this is the part that matters most, you will make it possible for others to do the same. Your growth will enable their growth. Your courage will fuel their courage. Your humanity will honor their humanity.

This is the real promise: You will become the kind of leader everyone desires. And in becoming that leader, you will help others become it too.

The Invitation

We invite you to join the movement. Not a formal organization or a certification program. A movement of leaders who refuse to keep walking the well-worn path. Who choose questions over answers. Who create space for thinking. Who tinker their way forward. Who learn, think, and experiment; publicly, persistently, and with others.

Leaders who understand that transformation happens through lived examples that others can follow. Through small dots, laid visibly, that invite others to add theirs. We invite you to lay your first dot this week. Tell us about it. Share it with a colleague. Post it where others can see. Not to brag but to teach. Not to perform but to invite. Your dot might be the permission someone else needs to lay theirs.

And when you lay that dot, you join a community of leaders scattered across organizations, sectors, and continents who are doing the same. Leaders who are choosing the harder, better path. Leaders who are transforming themselves and their organizations. Leaders who are living proof that there's another way to lead.

The Image That Was There All Along

Remember the connect-the-dots puzzle from our introduction? Here's what we've learned through our journey:

The image that was there all along. You just had to connect the dots to see it.

But there are deeper truths — the one Denise learned climbing up the steep hill in an unfamiliar country, the one Trisha found sitting in her office after another visit from her mentor asking her questions she couldn't answer, the one Sharon discovered after twenty seconds of silence, and the one Lucas experienced at 30,000 feet when "tell me more" accidentally became his leadership philosophy: you are following the dots and laying them.

Some dots have always been there, waiting to be noticed and connected. Others you are placing with each choice, each question, and each time you tinker. Your path has been uniquely yours. You are discovering who you already are while becoming who you need to be. The leader you are becoming will look different from the leaders we have become. And that is exactly as it should be.

But the truth we all arrive at is the same: Leadership is learning, thinking, and tinkering. The journey is continuous. The learning never ends. The cerebral highway stretches infinitely ahead. And that is not a problem to solve. That is the whole point.

So, we close not with a destination, but with an invitation to honor your readiness. To recognize that your learning will continue to unfold in its own rhythm and time. The journey continues. Your journey continues.

We gift you this: Be open to recognizing and honoring the natural rhythms of your growth, rather than pushing against them.

Now go and lay your first dot. Or your next one. Or pause and notice the dots beneath your feet.

With gratitude for sharing this journey with us,

Trisha, Denise, Michael, Sharon, Herminio, and Lucas

Notes (Our inspiration)

Book Cover:

Andy Magee- The pause symbol is represented by two vertical, parallel lines set against a sunset over ocean waves. These lines are echoed by two parallel rocks in the sea, bringing together a trinity of sun, sea, and land as metaphors for learners, thinkers, and tinkerers. It's an abstract interpretation of *pause and reflect* expressed through the mandala form.

Chapter One: The Stories That Shape Us

Peter, L. J., & Hull, R. (1994). *The peter principle*. Souvenir Press.

MARKU, A. (2023). *Smart goals mastery: Unlocking your potential and achieving success through smart goals.*

Chapter Five: Cultivating Conditions for Thought

Brooks, M. (Writer), Meehan, T. (Writer), & Stroman, S. (Director). (2001, April 19). *The Producers.* Live performance at the St. James Theatre.

Chapter Six: The Power of Thinking

Lebell, S. (2007). *The art of living: Epictetus—A new interpretation.* Harper One.

Chapter Seven: The Thinking Life

Coelho, P. (2014). *The Alchemist: A fable about following your dream* (25th anniversary ed.). Harper One. (Original work published 1988)

Follett, M. P. (2014). *The essential Mary Parker Follett: Ideas we need today* (J. D. Storey, Ed.). The Parliament Company.

Chapter Nine: Tinkerer Tenets

Wilkinson, K., & Petrich, M. (2014). *The art of tinkering: Meet 150+ makers working at the intersection of art, science & technology*. Weldon Owen.

Chapter Ten: The Tinkerer's Path

Collins, J., & Lazier, W. (2020). *BE 2.0 (Beyond entrepreneurship 2.0): Turning your business into an enduring great company*. Portfolio.

Handy, C. (1987). *Understanding voluntary organizations: How to make them function effectively*. Penguin UK.

Project Zero. (n.d.). *About*. Harvard Graduate School of Education.

Schein, E. H., & Schein, P. A. (2017). *Organizational culture and leadership* (5th ed.). John Wiley & Sons.

About the Authors

Trisha Beck, EdD, RN, NE-BC, FACHE

Weaving compassion with innovation, Trisha transforms spaces through a leadership style that places human stories at the center of every solution. Emerging from the frontlines of healthcare, she now orchestrates symphonies of connection where leadership and humanity dance in perfect rhythm rather than opposition. After more than two decades in the healthcare space, a Master's Degree from Northeastern University, and a Doctorate from New York University, Trisha strives to be like a bridge spanning the chasm between medicine and human dignity as she architects relationships that carry leaders toward a landscape where connection is the most powerful healing force of all.

Denise Nelson Nash, EdD, MFA, RYT-200

Denise's insatiable curiosity has propelled her through a constellation of careers, from the spotlight of the performing arts to the trenches of city administration, to the classrooms of academia, and into executive leadership. Grounded with a BA from Scripps College, a MFA from the University of Michigan, and a Doctorate from New York University—along with her 200-hour yoga teacher certification—she brings a rare blend of artistic vision, scholarly rigor, and mindful practice to her work. A self-proclaimed "professional Tinkerer," she has mastered the art of reinvention while maintaining her core philosophy of human-centered leadership. Her passport stamps are an integral part of her resume, with each global adventure adding new dimensions to her leadership lens. This book represents the crown jewel in Denise's treasure chest of collaboration; a culmination of lessons learned from boardrooms to backstages and everywhere in between.

Contributing Authors

Michael Miller, EdD, *The Learner*

At his core, Michael is a storyteller first—a truth that pulses through every dimension of his work and life. With a B.F.A. from New York University's Tisch School of the Arts, he approaches leadership through narrative, understanding that behind every policy and program lies a deeply human story. Over two decades in arts and higher education and a Doctorate from New York University, Michael has transformed rigid academic structures into flourishing ecosystems where authentic stories emerge and intersect. The collaborative spirit of theater has prepared him for the larger world, proving that true connection and innovation emerge when we weave together rigor, structure, humor, and understanding through storytelling.

Sharon Counts, EdD, *The Thinker*

Sharon's enduring belief in the arts as a catalyst for cultural transformation has guided her leadership across performance, education, and strategic design. As professor, producer, director, and storyteller, her work serves as both compass and canvas—orienting organizations toward equity while co-designing conditions for meaningful change. Her journey spans directing national productions and immersive Off-Broadway experiences to developing arts education programs creating access for thousands of New York City students and teachers. Now as Assistant Professor at Parsons School of Design, Sharon explores how design, innovation, and ethical leadership expand horizons of engagement—cultivating a civic and cultural landscape where creativity fuels connection and transformation.

Herminio L. Perez, DMD, MBA, EdD, *The Thinker*

Herminio considers himself a chronicler of life who happens to work in dentistry—though it took a dental degree (University of Medicine and Dentistry of New Jersey), a General Practice Residency in NYC, an MBA in Healthcare Systems (Fairleigh Dickinson University), and a doctorate in Education, Leadership, and Innovation (NYU Steinhardt) to realize that leadership isn't about having all the answers. These credentials weren't just boxes to check; they were his attempt to figure out how to bring humanity back into systems that too often forget the humans they're supposed to serve. When he's not working, you'll find him reading, listening to music, or writing—trying to make sense of what it means to lead authentically in a world that rewards performance. His approach to leadership is simple: ask better questions, listen more than you talk, and recognize that the best thing a leader can do is help people uncover what's already there.

Lucas Welter, EdD, *The Tinkerer*

Brazilian born, Lucas originally trained in architecture and urban planning before discovering his true blueprint wasn't made of concrete and steel but of people and systems. His curiosity about how communities thrive turned him into an architect of organizations. With a business degree from FGV São Paulo, a master's from the London School of Economics, and a doctorate from New York University, Lucas has spent over two decades with AFS Intercultural Programs, nurturing volunteer networks, helping individuals to become global citizens and leaders and driving organizational change across 60 countries. He teaches future change-makers, doctoral students at NYU Steinhardt, where theory meets practice (and a bit of joyful tinkering). Now proudly a Brooklynite, Lucas shares life—and plenty of design debates—with his partner, Andrew.

9 798994 764800